Building Community at Work

Advances in Community Psychology Series

The Book Series of the Society for Community Research and Action

Books in the Series

Principles of Social Change
Leonard A. Jason

Community Psychology and Community Mental Health: Towards Transformative Change
Edited by Geoffrey Nelson, Bret Kloos, and José Ornelas

Influencing Social Policy: Applied Psychology Serving the Public Interest
Kenneth I. Maton

Housing, Citizenship, and Communities for People With Serious Mental Illness: Theory, Research, Practice, and Policy Perspectives
Edited by John Sylvestre, Geoffrey Nelson, and Tim Aubry

Diverse Careers in Community Psychology
Edited by Judah J. Viola and Olya Glantsman

Community Power and Empowerment
Brian D. Christens

The Return of the Sun: Suicide and Reclamation Among Inuit of Arctic Canada
Michael J. Kral

Breaking Barriers: Sexual and Gender Minority-Led Advocacy to End AIDS in Africa and the Caribbean
Robin Lin Miller and George Ayala

Building Community at Work
Neil Boyd

Building Community at Work

Neil Boyd

OXFORD
UNIVERSITY PRESS

OXFORD
UNIVERSITY PRESS

Oxford University Press is a department of the University of Oxford.
It furthers the University's objective of excellence in research, scholarship,
and education by publishing worldwide. Oxford is a registered trademark of
Oxford University Press in the UK and in certain other countries.

Published in the United States of America by Oxford University Press
198 Madison Avenue, New York, NY 10016, United States of America.

Library of Congress Cataloging-in-Publication Data

Names: Boyd, Neil M., author.
Title: Building community at work / Neil Boyd.
Description: [New York] : [Oxford University Press], [2025] |
Series: Advances in community psychology series |
Includes bibliographical references and index.
Identifiers: LCCN 2024037508 (print) | LCCN 2024037509 (ebook) |
ISBN 9780197635933 (paperback) | ISBN 9780197635957 (epub) | ISBN 9780197635964
Subjects: LCSH: Psychology, Industrial. | Social psychology. | Community psychology.
Classification: LCC HF5548.8 .B677 2025 (print) | LCC HF5548.8 (ebook) |
DDC 158.7—dc23/eng/20241218
LC record available at https://lccn.loc.gov/2024037508
LC ebook record available at https://lccn.loc.gov/2024037509

DOI: 10.1093/9780197635964.001.0001

Printed by Marquis, Canada

MIX
Paper | Supporting
responsible forestry
FSC www.fsc.org FSC® C103567

Contents

Series Foreword

The Society for Community Research and Action (SCRA), Division 27 of the American Psychological Association, is an international and interdisciplinary organization that supports the development of theory, research, and social action. Members share a common interest in promoting empowerment, health, and well-being, with special attention to multiple levels of analysis, including the individual, group, organizational, community, cultural, and societal levels. Division members focus on an array of pressing social issues within national and global contexts (such as violence, mental health, HIV/AIDS, poverty, racism) and have developed, using a continuum of approaches from prevention to intervention and social change, effective social interventions to address seemingly intractable issues. These approaches to change involved diverse strategies, including, for example, advocacy, citizen participation, collaboration, community organizing, economic development, social movements, and policy change. These change strategies typically share the goal of challenging and altering underlying power structures in the pursuit of social justice and community and individual well-being.

This book series, Advances in Community Psychology, is sponsored by the SCRA and aims to aid in the dissemination of theory, research, and social action as developed by SCRA members as well as nonmembers working in allied disciplines. The overarching mission of the series is to create a publication venue that (a) highlights the contributions of the fields of community psychology and, more generally, community action, research, and practice; (b) integrates current knowledge regarding pressing topics and priorities for the field; and (c) offers the foundations for future directions.

This volume, *Building Community at Work*, provides an in-depth examination of psychological experiences of community within the workplace. Neil Boyd blends academic science with storytelling to demonstrate the importance of community and belonging for building thriving communities in organizations. The sense of belonging is a basic need for optimal human functioning, and psychological experiences of community becomes a barometer for a community's well-being. We live most, if not all, of our lives within communities; most of our time is spent in organizational communities and workplaces. The state of the workplace reflects the type of society it functions within. Several images and metaphors explain people's relationships to their workplace. Family, organism, machine: All are symbols of economic and social relations. One metaphor that speaks profoundly of our time is that of the psychic prison.

Psychic prisons conjure images of soulless production and worker disempowerment. Oppression is beyond the spectacles we witness; it becomes mundane and quotidian. People feel as if they repeatedly give up their souls and are forced to do horrible things in the name of profit. What does it say about our society when people view their workplaces as sites of psychological imprisonment? The mental carcerality of the workplace is an indicator of prevailing settler-colonial forms with modern-day neoliberal imperialist capitalism. Rather than serve as generators of well-being, many workplaces maintain hierarchical and exploitative capitalist–worker relations.

Consistently, workplaces are emblematic of a society's priorities. Who controls the means of production? How are workers treated in spaces of production? Is it surprising that a capitalist economic structure build-up through war, slavery, dispossession, and cultural destruction leaves those within it feeling enslaved or imprisoned? In the United States, an empire that has historically taken up the role of world policeman, a small class of capitalists view large areas of the world as their own mega-plantations for personal wealth generation and life extension. In discussing a psychological sense of community, Seymour Sarason remarked how corporations and governments use rhetoric to justify their imperialist expansion, an imperialist expansion that degrades a psychological sense of community.

The image of the psychic prison resonates strongly for many scholars of the African diaspora. The prison is a continuation and extension of the plantation as indicated by the 13th Amendment of the United States. The rhetoric of emancipation obscured the transformation and maintenance of a plantocratic epistemology and worldview. Black Codes and Jim Crow became legal frameworks, weapons of epistemological violence, that mark Africans as inherently deviant, barbaric, and criminal entities that needed to be managed, surveilled, or warehoused as surplus human capital. Imprisonment and slavery invoke the darkest parts of the human psyche. Such intergenerational trauma takes a physical and psychic toll on a group of people. When these imperial algorithms replicate across different spaces, the problem goes viral. What was once a psychic condition intentionally imposed on a defined racial Other becomes a democratized condition in which such feelings of psychological enslavement and conceptual incarceration threaten to overwhelm us no matter the sector. The logic of the rich being able to control and mistreat their employees is that of feudal lord over the serf, plantation owners over enslaved Africans and sharecroppers, and the colonizer over the colonized. This view of authority and power is an imperial algorithm and colonial meme rooted in domination rather than cooperation.

Building Community at Work implores us to move into a new era of human communities and workplaces in which everyone's psychological experience is equally valued. People want to build community at work; the existence of unions indicates people's willingness to build communities at work to ensure collective and individual well-being. The rise in union membership, louder critiques of the capitalist economic system, and more frequent strikes show that people will also build alternative communal structures when mainstream settings fail or are intentionally exploitative. The use of storytelling through vignettes is a way to humanize this discussion. While there will be the traditional discussion and citation of psychological concepts and frameworks, allow the story that unfolds to lead you through your own internal journal of community building. Envision yourself in the protagonist's position. What decisions would you have made similarly or differently? What stories do you have of your own community-building efforts? How can you help usher in a new era of organizational communities that are life generating instead of soul draining? How can we embody solidarity and a psychological sense of community?

Dominique Thomas
Book Series Editor

Acknowledgments

To my wife Victoria, who is my pole star for all things; to my daughter Anna, who is a constant reminder of the good in life; to my parents (Clarence and Ellen), my siblings (Craig, Krista, and Darryl), and mentors who showed me the way and pushed me to strive for a life worth living; and all of my extended family and friends who live in community with me. And, to Branda, who has shared a thirst for knowledge about experiences of community for the past 20 years.

Introduction

So why write a book about building community at work? This question has permeated my mind for quite some time, and there are both substantive and logistical answers that led to the creation of this effort. Let's start with some substance. The state of organizational life is quite varied across the globe from places where employees are treated well to places where corrupt practices exist and humans are treated as widgets under the control of authoritarian leadership. Gareth Morgan (1986) once noted that workplaces can be seen through the lens of various metaphors, and he opined that organizations can be viewed as machines, organisms, brains, cultures, political systems, and psychic prisons. All of these images of organizations have fascinated me throughout the years, but perhaps most vexing is the notion that many of us wake up in the morning and prepare ourselves for a day where we enter a psychic prison. What a sad notion this is, especially considering how much time we spend at work in our lives. Consider the fact that during a typical week in our working years, we wake up and spend 8 hours at work, come home and "relax" for 6–7 hours, go to bed for a similar amount of time, and do it all over again day in and day out.

A few years ago, the Covid-19 pandemic swept across the world, and the nature of work changed as many individuals experienced long hours at home working, while attempting to manage one's domestic affairs at the same time. Many of us were forced into our homes where work and homelife fully blurred and blended together, and escaping a difficult psychological setting was not possible or easy. And now as the pandemic has waned, we face a great resignation, quiet quitting, hybrid work roles (online and in-person), and a future of work that is forever changed. One could argue that the recent collective epiphany of not wanting to return to a prepandemic status quo work life is at least partially linked to a realization that many individuals want to escape the psychic prison of the brick-and-mortar office, or the working conditions of their previous job. Regardless of the new shift in how people want to work, the human condition in too many organizations is such that people wake up to a reality of some form of psychic prison every day, all in the name of making ends meet and providing for ourselves and our families. Some of us are more

Building Community at Work. Neil Boyd, Oxford University Press. © Oxford University Press (2025).
DOI: 10.1093/9780197635964.003.0001

fortunate than others, but if you are an employee, manager, or leader in an organization, I believe that you play a critical role in ameliorating the conditions that lead to settings where people feel like they are trapped.

Leaders, managers, and employees are an important audience of this book because you have direct effects on the psychological states of others in organizations, and you play a critical role in shaping their ability to experience community at work. A big part of the psychological trap is that workplaces often don't resemble settings where strong human-centered communities have been built. But don't worry; I think this book can help you see how to build communities at work that people want to "live" in.

This book is also intended as an academic manuscript for scholars and students in a variety of fields, including at its core community psychology, management, business administration, and public administration, and certainly nuanced fields like organizational behavior (the study of humans in organizations) and human resource management. However, I believe that the concepts, models, and theories of the book can apply to an enormous number of academic disciplines within the academy, and it contains information for learning, debate, critique, and analysis, and as a springboard for new scholarly explorations. I believe there are elements of this book that will appeal to both audiences at the same time and, on some occasions, appeal to perhaps just one of the audiences. I hope all of it digestible for everyone, but for example, if you are a management practitioner and you are reading something that sounds like it could be written in a peer-reviewed academic article, that's fine. Hang in there, keep reading, and I bet you'll learn something. If you're an academic and you are reading something that you think is intended for a practitioner audience, I think you will get something out of that too.

The concept of community has roots in many academic disciplines and can be visualized from a variety of lenses. Take the example of a political scientist who studies community through the lens of a nation-state, or the anthropologist who writes about an Indigenous community in midwestern Australia, or the geographer who details how the land has shaped activities of various communities over time. The writing contained in this book is focused on what I believe might be the most pressing and immediate form of community, a lens of community that never leaves us, and one that is omnipresent in our lives each day: the psychological state of community.

This book is about how we each psychologically experience community at work, a place where most of us spend incredible amounts of our time, and give our talent and energy, during our existence on earth. We can't escape our psychological experiences because they are inherent to our being no matter where we reside. One could argue that we might be able to leave a geographic community, or the community within a particular organization, but no matter where we traverse during this life, we cannot leave our psychological experiences. And, therefore, I believe it is imperative that leaders, managers, employees, scholars, and students understand the importance of community at work, understand their role in shaping a community at work, and strive to build better communities at work. Achieving these goals is not just a matter of crafting a community as an art form, but given my experience as a professor, consultant, and employee, it is a matter of science. The central thesis and arguments contained in this book are intended to help you understand the latest knowledge that is derived from management and psychological science, which will then need to be assimilated with the art of implementation by you no matter your role or location in an organization.

My journey toward an intellectual understanding of community at work began while I was a doctoral student completing a PhD in public administration at Penn State; however, because I had previously completed advanced degrees in psychology (BA—Bloomsburg University, MA—University of Notre Dame) and business administration (MBA—Penn State), it is clear that I have been interested in the psychological issues of employees for a long time. During my doctoral studies, I was teaching research methods and industrial psychology courses in a behavioral sciences department at Penn State, and the department had a master's degree program in community psychology. Immersion and conversations with department members Bob Coleman, Clem Gilpin, Kamini Grahame, and especially Holly Angelique led me to the realization that the fields of community psychology and organization studies (i.e., management and public administration) had intellectual similarities and convergence.

There were many points of convergence, but a few that stood out to me at the time were that both fields had similar intellectual roots around change processes (i.e., Kurt Lewin in relation to community and organizational change), a shared desire and application of theory at the macro unit of analysis (e.g., systems, chaos, ecological, institutional) and micro unit of analysis (e.g., psychological approaches of cognition, behaviorism, humanism), and several key tenets that were present in each field (e.g., prevention, empowerment, systems-ecological analysis, social justice, a concern for marginalized individuals). That led me to choose community psychology as a subfield in my doctoral program where Clem Gilpin and Holly Angelique served on my comprehensive exam committee, and Holly Angelique later served on my dissertation committee.

Because of my interest in the intersection of community psychology and organization studies, a comprehensive exam question and answer related to the intersection of the fields led to one of my early publications, coauthored with Holly Angelique, titled "Rekindling the Discourse: Organization Studies in Community Psychology," published in the *Journal of Community Psychology* (Boyd and Angelique, 2002). The study was constructed as a follow-up to the work of Keys and Frank (June 1987) who shepherded a special issue in the *American Journal of Community Psychology* that was dedicated to organizational concerns. Keys and Frank asked two main questions in their lead article:

(1) What does community psychology contribute to the study of organizations, and (2) what does the study of organizations contribute to community psychology? We conducted a content analysis of studies published in the *American Journal of Community Psychology* and *Journal of Community Psychology* from 1977 through the end of 2000, and we found that organization constructs and theories were modestly utilized by community psychologists, and therefore we argued for a strengthening of the relationship between the fields.

Our work was also influenced by recent remarks of Meg Bond during her 1998 presidential address to the Society for Community Research and Action (Division 27 of the American Psychological Association; Scra27.org) in which she proclaimed, "The central settings in most adults' lives are the organizations in which they work, study, pursue shared interests, and become involved in community concerns." In 2007, Holly and I partnered to shepherd a second special issue in the *Journal of Community Psychology* titled "Resuming the Dialogue on Organization Studies and Community Psychology" (Boyd and Angelique, 2007). In 2011, I edited a special issue for the *Journal of Prevention and Intervention in the Community*, on a more nuanced topic that focused on organization development in community contexts (Boyd, 2011a), and in 2014, I conducted a follow-up to the 2002 article titled "A Ten-Year Retrospective of Organization Studies in Community Psychology: Content, Theory, and Impact," also published in the *Journal of Community Psychology* (Boyd, 2014). In the 2014 retrospective article, I noted that since 2002, a number of events had marked a renewed interest in the intersection between community psychology and organization studies.

Besides the special issues that brought focused attention of the intersection of organization studies and community psychology in the academic literature, a series of conference symposia and presentations were delivered at Society for Community Research and Action biennials (e.g., Boyd, 2009; Boyd and Nowell, 2011; Boyd et al., 2007), Academy of Management meetings (e.g., Boyd et al., 2009; Tschirhart et al., 2010), and the Southeastern Ecological and Community Psychology Conference (Nowell et al., 2012). Further, I shepherded the creation of an organization studies interest group in the Society for Community Action and Research, and a series of single article publications had appeared in community psychology journals focusing on organization studies topics such as appreciative inquiry and organization development (Bess, Prilleltensky, Perkins, and Collins, 2009; Boyd, 2011b; Boyd and Bright, 2007; Perkins et al., 2007), and transorganizational networks (Nowell, 2009). A decade ago, it was clear that the organization studies literature in community psychology had significantly increased since 2000. Community psychologists had enhanced their scholarly presence in organizational settings, they had applied a greater number of organization concepts in their work, and they more often used organization models and theory as explanatory frameworks in their studies. In addition, community psychologists had attempted to bridge the gap with organization scholars through conference presentations and publications in organization studies venues.

My intellectual development at the intersection of organization studies and community psychology was also heavily influenced by a chance meeting with Branda Nowell in Pasadena, California, in 2007. I had finished my PhD in public administration and was an assistant professor in the business administration department at Lycoming College in Williamsport, Pennsylvania (the home of Little League Baseball). I was in the early stages of an academic career after working as a management consultant for over 15 years, and I was fortunate to meet Branda, who was a newly minted PhD from Michigan State in community psychology beginning her first academic appointment in a public administration program at North Carolina State. We were both attending the biennial Society for Community Action and Research Conference, and after attending a conference panel where one of us was presenting, we decided to have lunch. During our time together, it was uncanny how much we had in common at the intersection of community psychology and organization studies.

Our conversation led to what is almost now a 20-year collaboration, but at that time and space, it became clear that we had two central collective interests. We were equally fascinated by concepts, models, and theories in the field of community psychology and management / public administration, and we agreed that more scholars should explore the fruitful boundary space between the disciplines. Community psychologists were actively studying concepts such as empowerment, ecological analysis and systems theory, prevention, social justice, community and social change, diversity, and a psychological sense of community. Management scholars were also studying these concepts (sometimes under a different name), or studying related constructs, and it was clear to us that there were plenty of unique ideas from each field that could be translated and studied across the boundaries of the disciplines (e.g., participatory action research as an organization development and change approach, appreciative inquiry as a management consulting process in social change settings).

As an opening act, we decided to explore the concept of a psychological sense of community that had been the brainchild of Seymour Sarason at Yale in the 1970s (Sarason, 1974). A decade later, David McMillan and David Chavis at Vanderbilt had extended the work of Sarason by articulating that a *sense of community* is composed of *membership*, *need fulfillment*, *influence*, and *shared emotional connection*, which set the stage for the first measurement scheme of the construct (McMillan and Chavis, 1986). Since the publication of their seminal work, scholars in the field of community psychology have conducted many studies that employed the McMillan and Chavis framework. However, our initial literature search in the fields of management and public management led to a somewhat shocking discovery. We could barely find a trace of research and conversation about community at work. This discovery was equally shocking because of the inherent interdisciplinary nature of management research (especially with the social sciences), and because we fully expected that someone must be studying this important issue. In the parlance of a researcher, a big wide research gap was in front of us, and therefore we decided to begin a study of community at work.

As you will see in greater detail soon, our synchronized dive into the pool of this research gap led us toward attempts of conceptualizing a sense of community at work, trying to develop underlying assumptions and theory that explained how and why a psychological sense of community develops in organizational settings, and designing and running empirical research studies to test if a sense of community was unique from other long-studied management and public management constructs, and to determine if a sense of community predicted important employee outcomes. Our first efforts helped to create conceptual clarity, and our early qualitative work suggested that multiple constructs are present when individuals have what we now call *community experiences at work*. We learned that a psychological sense of community is created when particular relational needs are met (membership, influence, shared emotional connection; aka the McMillan and Chavis model), and when individuals experience a *sense of community responsibility* (a new discovery of ours).

Next, we developed a measurement scale for a sense of community responsibility, and we learned that a sense of community and a sense of responsibility are empirically unique constructs, and they tend to predict different individual cognitive, emotional, and behavioral outcomes. Further work suggested that community experiences are powerful measures for a host of important individual outcomes at work, and that community constructs appeared to be better at predicting those outcomes compared with state-of-the-art management and public management constructs that had existed in the literature for decades. Our latest work has shown that certain features in the context of an organization can lead to the development of community at work, and we have shown that community experiences are transferable to any collective experience (i.e., work, home, clubs, teams, classrooms, friend groups, etc.). Our work has also been supported and augmented by other researchers in recent years, as you will soon learn, and we have separately explored other areas of connection between the fields of community psychology and organization studies (e.g., appreciative inquiry, thriving at work, network organizations, disaster management).

In addition to my scholarship, which was conducted as a faculty member with research and teaching and responsibilities at several universities (previously at Penn State and Lycoming College), I am currently a professor of management and the chair of the Management & Organizations Department at Bucknell University. Upon my arrival to Bucknell in 2013, I was immediately able to incorporate psychological experiences of community into several courses (i.e., Introduction to Organization & Management and Human

Resource Management), and I joined a faculty group who had an ethos that embraced social, environmental, and economic justice as frames by which we should educate management students. I write about some of my teaching experiences later in the book, but I would like to note that my presence stimulated an additional focus that community at work matters in organizations, and I was (and still am) in a faculty group that greatly respected interdisciplinary research explorations that advanced knowledge in the field of management (including public management), and enhanced our ability to teach students how to critically think, organize, and manage for a sustainable and just world.

Finally, in addition to my academic pursuits, I have worked as a management consultant since the early 1990s. My early career mostly focused on human resource management consulting in designing recruiting, hiring, performance appraisal, training, and other humancentric systems, and organizational behavior consulting in the development of employee reward and recognition systems, wellness programs, and the measurement of psychological states of employees. Over many years of consulting, my portfolio of topics grew to include areas like strategic planning, board development, structural change, and infusing sustainable management into organizations, and as my scholarship on psychological experiences of community grew, I added it to my consulting toolbelt in helping organizations change as a scientist-practitioner. As you will see later in the book, the concept of community at work is applicable to macro units of analysis in organizations (e.g., boards of directors, top executive teams, strategic management), meso units (e.g., departments and division of human resource management, marketing, accounting and finance, operations, etc.), and micro units (e.g., individuals and small groups within organizations). And, my commentaries throughout the book are created by all of my collective experiences as a consultant, educator, and research scholar.

In my view, the understanding of community at work has matured, and I am confident that scientific knowledge has progressed to a point where we have enough evidence about community experiences at work to write a book-length manuscript. Science is our guide, and yes, science is not always swift, but I hope that by grounding my words in the accumulation of science over the past two decades it will give you comfort and confidence that this book is the best I can provide at the moment in terms of understanding how to study psychological experiences of community and how to build communities at work.

In designing the structure of the book, I have carefully thought about how to engage and immerse you in knowledge about community at work. That's why the book begins with a story. A story? you ask. Just give me the facts, you might be thinking. If you're looking for facts, don't put the book down yet; I'll provide many of them, and in addition, I will share concepts, models, and theory from academic science. However, I start each chapter with a very short story in the form of a novella that progresses the reader along the journey of someone who is trying to understand how to build community. In my years as an educator and scholar, I have learned that stories can tell more than a thousand words. Think about all of the situations where stories are used. We love to listen to stories about our parents and grandparents. Many of the popular television shows we watch are story based. When reading for pleasure, most people turn to fiction because they can embed themselves in the intrigue of the story. In my classes, I notice that students perk up when I lead a sentence with "let me tell you a story." In the academic world, storytelling as a method of teaching has grown significantly in the past few decades and has become (to many) a legitimate form of engaging students in class (Landrum, Brakke, and McCarthy, 2019). I often employ this practice in my classes by having students listen to professionals who can regale them with stories from the street, or I have students tell stories about specific experiences they had in organizations, and I then help interpret how to analyze what is happening in the world via academic concepts, models, and theory.

Storytelling is a method that, today, is part of providing engaged experiences in academic settings. In the early days of being a professor, I often used textbooks and lengthy academic manuscripts in my undergraduate courses. I still use a lot of academic sources in my classes (especially shorter ones), but several years ago a faculty colleague turned me on to *Let My People Go Surfing* by Yvon Chouinard, the founder of Patagonia (Chouinard, 2016). The book is a treatise on Yvon's journey in creating an organization as a reluctant businessman, and in short, the book is a story of how the company was formed and grew to become what it is today. It was the first book I ever used in a course where students consistently said, "We loved that book, and reading it was interesting and fun." Since that time, I have used books to tell stories of organizational life, and they have worked well to keep my students engaged and able to have contextual information that we can link to data, science, and knowledge in our fields of academic study.

I hope you feel the same way as you follow the journey of Amanda, a fictional character, who, like many of us, is on a journey to discover how to pay attention to and build community at work. Amanda is a young executive who is running an apparel company that has quickly grown and expanded its products into a variety of garment offerings. I think the story of a young executive and her journey in learning about how to build a community at work will be an engaging way to help you see what it takes to move the needle from "not quite understanding what to do" to "fully getting it" in relation to being a leader who is committed to designing community experiences in organizations. You will notice that I intentionally attempt to weave the story with academic discourse, and at times I completely separate them. It was a challenge to write this way, but I did this with a hope that you find the book engaging and helpful to you no matter your vantage point . . . whether that be a leader, manager, or employee in an organization, or a scholar and student in fields like community psychology, management, public administration, organizational behavior, human resource management, or others.

I hope you also notice that there are a variety of manifest thoughts and actions of Amanda (and those around her) that I directly analyze and critique, and a series of cognitive and behavioral outcroppings that I intentionally leave for you to interpret. I do this because I have found it useful for scholars, students, and organizational practitioners to have intellectual freedom of interpretation beyond the specific intent of a writer, and to especially give you a capability to interpret and analyze manifest and latent content through your own intellectual and academic lenses. I expect, for example, that a community psychologist might find some intellectual nuggets that an organizational behavior scholar might not (and vice versa), and I believe that practicing managers might interpret something differently than a newly graduated student from an MBA program. If you find something that makes you smile, or murmur "hmmmm," that's great. If you find something that irks you about a character, or the way I situate them, that's great too. All of it is up for individual interpretation and critique.

I also want to explain why I position *Amanda's Journey* within a private-sector company instead of some other organizational form. I wholeheartedly believe, and the science in this area shows, that experiencing community at work and building it are ubiquitous to any organizational form (public, nonprofit, private sector organizations, grassroots, cooperatives, etc.). However, conservative estimates show that approximately 70% of employees in the United States work in private sector organizations, and therefore it made sense to me to create a story that was most common to humans in organizational settings (at least in the United States where I reside). Community psychologists are most likely less familiar with private sector settings, as much of their work is based in community settings and their direct or indirect connection with nonprofit and government organizations, but as I have noted in various presentations and publications over the years, the private sector is clearly a place where community psychology concepts, models, theory, and practices *can* and *should* be applied. In other words, we need more community psychologists, and community psychology thinking, in private sector organizations. Management practitioners and scholars will have little challenge in relating to a company as an organizational setting, but I believe they will find other ideas that nudge them out of their comfort zones. I expect that will be true for all who read this book . . . that you will find things that fully resonate from your vantage point, and other ideas that give you pause and an opportunity for reflection and analysis.

In Chapter 1, "Amanda's Journey Begins and the Concept of Community Origins and History," I begin with an exploration of the concept of community and trace its historical roots across various fields where it has been defined in different ways. As the chapter progresses, I will show you how community can be a macro- and micro-oriented construct, and I will demonstrate that paying attention to, and measuring, community experiences (at the micro level) is an important endeavor for managers, leaders, and employees. I will show how our work on psychological sense of community and a sense of community responsibility intersects with multiple fields of study, how it is a relatively new set of constructs in the management literature, and how the science of community has developed in recent years.

In Chapter 2, "Life Is Great and the Community Imperative," we follow Amanda's journey where she is deeply entrenched in "old school" single-bottom-line management thinking where efficiency and profitability are the key tenets of her organization. On the surface, life is great for Amanda, but an undercurrent of problems will eventually lead her to begin a process of introspection toward understanding community at work. The chapter then turns to academic and professional considerations of the importance of community at work. Large numbers of employees are unhappy with their work and work contexts. People are searching for ways to live fulfilling lives in organizations. Many managers are searching for ways to stimulate production and employee well-being and satisfaction. Popular press literature is calling for the development of communities at work. Scholars are highlighting issues with class, race, gender, and diversity/inclusion. Recent scholarship has caught up to these calls, and a new science of community at work exists to help managers and employees reach their goals. Developing communities at work is an important activity that managers need to consider, and the chapter will connect back to elements of Amanda's story along the way to help you see a variety of issues that are embedded in the concepts and models of community experience.

In Chapter 3, "It's Not All Roses and Defining and Measuring Community at Work," a series of employee rumblings push Amanda and her executive team to find out what is wrong in the organization. However, their attempts to understand the root problems ends in a situation where they still don't get it. We then turn to the *community experience model* and how scholars define and measure community at work. Community experiences are grounded in what organizations can give to employees (a need fulfillment notion) and what members of organizations can give to others and the workplace as a whole (a responsibility notion). A variety of metrics exist, and a few are starting to be used in organizational settings. By exploring these measures, one can develop a way to find out the current state of the community at work. Again, the chapter will connect back to elements of Amanda's story along the way to help you see a variety of issues that are embedded in the concepts and models of community experience.

In Chapter 4, "Seeking Help and Planning to Build Community," after struggling with how to find the help, Amanda will decide to hire in a consultant (Susan) who will assist in developing a culture of community in the organization. We will learn how Amanda and the consultant work together to execute their organization development and change plan, and how it ultimately leads to the company achieving a culture of community. We will see Amanda's worldviews change, and how that helps her take the appropriate steps forward.

Amanda will also develop an appreciation for community-related concepts, models, and theory (partly because it fits with her linear thinking), and she will experience positive outcomes and learn lessons about various interventions that ultimately build community in her organization. The chapter then briefly explores steps toward planning how to create communities at work and shares practical insights on how employees and managers can move forward with planning. The chapter will highlight recent scientific investigations that are helping us to understand how we can shape a better future where employees can experience thriving lives at work, and where managers can satisfy goals under their charge.

In Chapter 5, "Putting It All Together and Building Community," you will explore how Amanda's journey is akin to our own personal journey. You may or may not be in the same place as Amanda when she begins her story, but all of us are somewhere between "not getting it at all" to "fully getting it" in terms of promoting and developing communities at work. We are all agents of change at work, and in our academic scholarship endeavors, and we can do things in various aspects of our work to help build community. We can do things by the ways we act at work, by formal interventions in our jobs and work units, in the techniques we use as managers and leaders, and in the executive suite of the organization. And we can engage in academic learning and research in a search for a greater understanding of community in the many organizational forms that we traverse. The chapter will finish as a sort of "call to action" for all of us to do our part in bringing needed community psychology principles and theories to the private sector (and all organizational forms), and to strive toward building strong communities at work.

I hope you read onward with a joy for learning, exploration, and inspiration, because my journey has been nothing short of the same!

Neil

CHAPTER 1

Amanda's Journey Begins and the Concept of Community

Origins and History

AMANDA'S JOURNEY BEGINS

It's 6:30 a.m. on Monday, and Amanda is already moving quickly about her bedroom getting ready for work. Two cups of coffee are helping to fuel her fast pace, and she is mentally working through her talking points for a meeting she has at 8:00 a.m. this morning. Her mind is running through notes to self: quarterly profits are up 1.3% in the same period compared with past years, employee production has been steady, and a new efficiency software has increased the rate of call speed by 15% in the customer service department. She's particularly worried about Jim, a board member, who constantly questions earnings potential, so her mind is mostly fixated on anticipating his questions. In the back of her mind, she anticipates a series of queries about a new branding rollout for a spring apparel line next year, and, again, most of her concern is related to how she will be able to pitch the return on investment of the expenditures.

Just then, she hears a knock on the door. It's her three-and-a-half-year-old daughter, Gabby, who says, "Mommy, pancakes." "In a minute," she says, gazing into the bathroom mirror as she hastily applies her eyeliner. Gabby runs out of the room, and you can hear her yell downstairs, "Mommy's coming, Daddy."

Ten minutes later, Amanda is throwing her cell phone and glasses into her purse as she rushes downstairs to greet her family. As she enters the kitchen, she sees her husband, Ken, with spatula in hand over the griddle; daughter, Gabby, waiting patiently at the table; and her 10-week-old baby boy, Jensen, reclining in his portable baby chair. "I'm sorry, honey, what's for breakfast?" "Ummm, it's OK I guess," Ken says sarcastically. "Blueberry pancakes. Orange

Building Community at Work. Neil Boyd, Oxford University Press. © Oxford University Press (2025).
DOI: 10.1093/9780197635964.003.0002

juice is in the fridge. Busy day today?" "That's an understatement," she says. She pours a small glass of orange juice, and on her way to the table she gives Jensen a smooch on the forehead. "Ahhhh, it's gonna be a long day. I have a big meeting all morning, and a variety of staff meetings in the afternoon." While Ken is plating Gabby's food, she catches herself staring at the backyard, thinking about the most recent earnings data. She snaps her head back to see Gabby looking right at her. "You OK mommy?" Gabby asks. "Yes, sweetie, I'm fine," she says, as she tries to hide the deep sigh she was about to take.

By all accounts Amanda's life has been great. She is 35 years old, and a successful entrepreneur who is running an apparel company that has grown by leaps and bounds in the past 8 years. She graduated from one of the best fashion and design institutes in the United States, and after launching her brand in her early 20s, she decided to get an MBA at a prestigious school in the city while she continued to run the business. She "needed" the MBA even though she had taken management courses during her undergrad days because, in her words, she "was more into her design courses back then." She heeded some good advice from a professor in her first semester who encouraged her to develop her weaknesses, which led her to focus on accounting and finance as concentration areas. She struggled with the material but tried not to let it show—not even to her family. After graduation, she felt relief that the double life of a student and business owner would settle down, and in some ways it did, but then life brought new turns and challenges.

One night when she was out with friends at a restaurant, which she was hardly able to do, she met Ken, who was passing by their table while on a walk with his Bernese mountain dog named Benny. He was handsome and chatty, and she could tell he was artsy. In fact, they attended the same school, but he was 2 years behind her and they had never met. He had a passion for photography, especially physical landscapes that explored the human condition, and he always had a camera by his side. In fact, on the night they met, he took a picture of the group and texted it to Amanda later that night. That's how their relationship developed, by a chance encounter on the street with the medium of photography as their connection. Quickly they were spiritually inseparable, but because of her work demands, they weren't able to spend as much time together as they wanted. Instead, they mostly stayed connected by video messages, social media, and lots of endearing texts back and forth. In the early days, they were able to see each other a couple of times per week, but as things progressed, Ken became impatient and would ask to stay over so they could be together more. Her life always seemed to be a balancing act between work, Ken, attempts to keep friends, and the occasional activity that would allow her to escape. Her go-to escape was running, and it allowed her to block out most of the world and at the same time engage in critical thinking. But that was before marriage, and shortly after, the birth of Gabby. Once Gabby graced their lives, the balancing act became more of a juggling act with 10 balls in the air, but

Amanda was strong and committed and could handle anything. That's how she was raised: to get up and keep going when the chips were down. And, nothing was going to stop her from living a charmed life.

THE CONCEPT OF COMMUNITY: ORIGINS AND HISTORY

As Amanda's journey begins, we see the image of a young professional who, by most Western societal standards, is successful. She is running a profitable business, she graduated from excellent universities, she has a beautiful family, and she's balancing the demands of life. Some might even say she is a superwoman! Others might question if she's truly happy and content in the organizational domains through which she traverses.

Those of us who study organizations as a phenomenon conceptualize humans as they move from one collective to another in what we might call "organizational communities" (Boyd and Angelique, 2002). When Amanda woke up this morning, she was in the community of her family, and she is about to leave the house and enter the community of her workplace. And, in both of these communities, she has primary responsibilities for creating the cultures of community. After work, she plans to head to the gym, where she will join a community of athletes, fitness experts, and individuals who are trying to stay active and healthy. And, depending on the day of the week, she occasionally engages with a community in her neighborhood, and various communities that define our "third place" social scenes (e.g., restaurants, theaters, shops, clubs; see Zipay, Pychlau, and Wagner, 2020). A distinction here is that a place can be defined as a community, while others might focus on the culture or social exchange process within a particular place as a community. For now, I may interchangeably use the terms *community* and *collectives*, but as you will soon see, the working definition of *community* for this book will primarily focus on the psychological process of experiencing community within a particular place (i.e., the workplace). However, such a focus does not take away from the variety of ways that scholars conceptualize the construct of community.

Our navigation through various communities is an interesting characteristic of the human experience, and one that requires social exchange in ways that are mutually beneficial to stakeholders in the collective setting. We often ignore the journey through various collectives and compartmentalize our experiences in these communities. For example, we experience collectives with seemingly very specific referents: my family, my workplace, my soccer team, my favorite ice cream shop. And yet, our experiences in these communities are not entirely discrete. Amanda's morning interaction with her family will carry into her drive to work, which will intersect with the beginning of her workday. The successes, trials, and tribulations of a workday will impact her workout at the gym, and perhaps all of her daily experiences with others will drive how she interacts with her family once she arrives home at night. In short, our experiences of community are more like a stream of consciousness than a set of distinct acts in distinct settings. The realization of the fluidity of community experiences, and their intersection with separate physical and socially constructed spaces, is something that has interested scholars as they have attempted to define and characterize the concept of community.

The concept of community is at least as old as the formation of species within our universe. Ecologists note that community refers to the coexistence of similar or disparate species in a specific place and time (Mittelbach and McGill, 2019). The assemblage of interacting organisms dynamically alters their abundance, dispersion, and adaptation, and central components of ecological community include their collective structure and function. An ecological community can range from a small assemblage on a tree to the species relationships in the global biome. The logic of communities within communities is similar to the early Greek philosophers who saw the polis as containing political, social, and economic elements. In the classic Greek philosophical interpretation of the polis, the concept of community (i.e., social interaction) was intertwined and engrained with political and economic relations between people, and by the Age of Enlightenment (late 1700s–early 1800s), community and society were interchangeable concepts. For Rousseau in the 18th century, civil society was grounded in the concept of the polis, where humans could flourish with individual autonomy and relate to the state toward goals that promoted the common good (Bertram, 2004). The concept of community involved the entity of the state and yet at the same time included the proximate social relations that humans experienced in their physical geographic communities and within their homes. While some writers of the 17th and 18th centuries challenged the notion that community and the state could peacefully coexist, in 1976, Seymour Sarason, a well-known psychologist who helped to facilitate the genesis of the field of community psychology, clearly pronounced a tension between the two by stating, "The more powerful the state becomes, the more its people look to it as the fount of initiative and succor, the more is the psychological sense of community diluted" (Sarason, 1976, p. 251). He further argued that when the lives of people are a consequence of decisions made by the state, they tend to be robbed of those communal bonds and responsibility upon which a sense of community is built. In short, Sarason was not convinced that state entities could produce contextual conditions that give human beings the freedom to freely associate and create community. As such, his notion of community was not reliant on any entity of the state for its creation. In a related way, the South African philosophy of Ubuntu is an interesting notion for conceptualizing humanity as defined by a collective. Seen by many as the defining principle in numerous African societies, Ubuntu is characterized as the principle that our personhood depends on our relationship with others: "A person is a person through other persons"—*Mutu ke mutu ka batho*, as the Basotho say. Or, in Swahili, it is captured through the axiom *Mutu ni utu*, meaning "a human being is humanity" (Kresse, 2007, p. 139; Ogude and Dyer, 2019). Wilson and Williams (2013) characterize Ubuntu as the notion that we are people because of other people, and that we are people because of other people recognizing the need for connecting with others. Nobles, Baloyi, and Sodi (2016) further note that a person does not become a person in isolation as an individual but, rather, through participation and engagement in a community of persons. Recent scholarship by community psychologists affirms these notions in exploring the colonialism of a Westernized community psychology (Beals et al., 2021), by noting that Ubuntu is a philosophy that centralizes community and emphasizes relationality with all dimensions of existence without the interference and need of the nation-state.

Therefore, it is clear that definitions of community are varied (see Table 1.1). Some conceptualizations focus on functional outcomes like adaptation and survival as species congregate in an ecological location, while others center on social interaction and their relation with socially constructed systems (e.g., political, economic) that are bounded within, and perhaps as a function of, the nation-state. African philosophy presents us with an alternative view and reminds us that community is bounded by people, for people, as a central purpose of humanity and personhood. Debates on the concept of community continue today, but as we consider the nature of community as it relates to human interaction, it is important to remember that people reside and function within some form of a bounded space. As geographers of "place studies" note, community happens in a location. The location can be as large as the globe or nation, intermediate in size like a city or town, and immediate like your neighborhood, online gaming community, a small group that organically forms, or the places where we work. Within those spaces, individuals form identities of personhood, interact, commiserate, express themselves, bond with each other, and love.

The premise of this book focuses on both of these elements: the human experience of community that occurs in relation to other individuals, and a specific location, that is, the workplace. Further, the treatise here is especially focused on the psychological nature of community, which is the most proximal form of community that can be conceived. The location, or place, of community is important, as are its structure and function. However, I assert that the daily psychological experience of community is most pressing to our human existence. We cannot escape our psychological experiences of community, and they are fundamental to every collective place and structure that we experience.

Table 1.1 A FEW CONCEPTUALIZATIONS OF COMMUNITY

Reference point	Form	Function
Ecology	Species in a specific place and time	Survival, adaptation
Greek philosophy	Polis	Social, political, economic interaction
Enlightenment philosophy	Civil society/nation-state	Social contract with the state toward the common good
African philosophy	Ubuntu: Human collectives are humanity.	Personhood happens by interaction in collectives.
Geography	Place	A bounded location for community

The Roots of a Psychological Focus on Community

The psychological nature of community can be directly traced to the early work of Seymour Sarason. In 1974, he pronounced that the study of a *psychological sense of community* should be the defining concept for the budding field of community psychology. In his seminal book, Sarason described a sense of community as ". . . the sense that one was part of a readily available mutually supportive network of relationships upon which one could depend, and as a result of which one did not experience sustained feelings of loneliness. . ." (p. 1). After Sarason's call to study a psychological sense of community, scholars began to empirically assess a sense of community in a variety of settings (Doolittle and MacDonald, 1978; Glynn, 1981; Riger and Lavrakas, 1981).

In now what is regarded as an inflection point in the study of psychological sense of community research, McMillan and Chavis (1986) posited that a sense of community has four subcomponents: (a) *membership*—a feeling of belonging or of sharing a sense of personal relatedness; (b) *influence*—a sense of mattering, of making a difference to a group, and of the group mattering to its members; (c) *integration and fulfillment of needs*—a feeling that member's needs will be met by the resources received through their membership in the group; and (d) *shared emotional connection*—the commitment and belief that members have shared and will share history, common places, time together, and similar experiences (p. 9).

Since 1986, it is clear that the McMillan and Chavis (1986) framework has played a dominant role in the literature on sense of community. Using the framework, researchers have shown that a sense of community correlates with various indicators of well-being, including life satisfaction (e.g., Pretty et al., 1996; Prezza, Amici, Roberti, and Tedeschi, 2001), perceptions of belonging and community connectedness (e.g., Sonn, 2002; Sonn and Fisher, 1996), mental health symptoms (Ellaway, Macintyre, and Kearns, 2001), and loneliness (Pretty, Andrews, and Collet, 1994). A sense of community has been shown to correlate with community involvement types of behaviors such as participation in a community (e.g., Chavis and Wandersman, 1990), political participation (e.g., Hughey, Speer, and Peterson, 1999), and intention to stay in residence (e.g., Perkins et al., 1990). A sense of community has been studied in many social settings, including religious communities (Miers and Fisher, 2002), immigrant communities (Sonn, 2002), student communities (Pretty, 1990), Internet communities (Obst, Zinkiewicz, and Smith, 2002), residential and geographic communities (Brodsky, O'Campo, and Aronson, 1999; Perkins et al., 1990), and even within the workplace (Cantano, Pretty, Southwell, and Cole, 1993; Mahan, 2000; Pretty and McCarthy, 1991; Pretty, McCarthy, and Catano, 1992).

To the best of my knowledge, Klein and D'Aunno (1986) were the first to discuss a sense of community at work when they developed an exploratory framework for the study of a psychological sense of community in the workplace (PSCW). They noted that community psychologists to date had only studied a sense of community in delimited geographic areas or neighborhoods, and they argued that we needed to better understand experiences of community in organizational settings given how much time we spend at work. They expressed three important components in their model, (1) factors hypothesized to influence or determine a sense of community in the workplace (e.g., individual employee, job, leaders, work group, organizational, extra-organizational characteristics), (2) referents or anchor points for individuals' sense of community (i.e., friendship network, functional subgroup, whole organization, profession–job class–union, work site–community), and (3) mechanisms that underlie and explain the relationship between the hypothesized determinants and sense of community (i.e., formation of a community identity, positive appraisal of the group and desire to become a member, active involvement in the group). Their work highlighted that a sense of community at work is influenced by antecedents within individuals and the context of the organization, cognitive and behavioral mechanisms of the individual, and that a sense of community could apply to various referents from macro (e.g., the whole organization) to micro (e.g., friendship network) units of analysis.

However, over the next two decades, workplace studies that focused on a sense of community were loosely scattered across the community psychology literature. For example, Pretty and McCarthy (1991) explored whether a psychological sense of community could be predicted by characteristics of the psychosocial climate. They found that work environment factors acted differently for men and women. Male managers' sense of community was predicted by their perceptions of peer cohesion and involvement, whereas female managers' sense of community was predicted by their perceptions of supervisor support, involvement, and work pressure. Their study is a good example of antecedents, or factors in the organizational context, that could influence the development of a sense of community. A few years later, Royal and Rossi (1996) conducted a study on sense of community that included employed adults. They found that a sense of community was positively related to organizational attachment, job satisfaction, and role clarity, and negatively related to intentions to leave the organization, role conflict, role overload, and psychological distress. Their work showed that a sense of community could lead to individual outcomes that had implications for employees and the organization.

In 1998, Burroughs and Eby attempted to operationalize the construct of PSCW. They developed a measurement system and tested an initial framework of antecedents and consequences. They showed that antecedents of PSCW were needed for affiliation, organizational tenure, size of work group, employee acquaintances, transactional psychological contracts, and relational psychological contracts, and they determined that possible outcomes of PSCW were job satisfaction and organizational citizenship behavior. While certainly not exhaustive of the entire set of scattered studies into the 2000s (see Boyd and Angelique, 2002, and Boyd, 2014, for all organization-related studies from 1977 to 2011), it is clear that community psychologists expressed a constant slow simmering of intellectual activity in this space for some time. It is also clear that most of the studies and discussions of a sense of community at work had focused on attempts to translate measures from known sense of community scales, invent new measures for of a sense of community at work, investigate antecedents and outcomes of a sense of community, and discuss the importance of organizational settings as locations to understand a sense of community.

Origins of Change: Community at Work Reimagined

A new inflection point emerged in the academic literature in 2010, when Branda and I challenged the theoretical underpinnings and measurement schemes of a sense of community (Nowell and Boyd, 2010). We were attempting to understand if a sense of community mattered in work settings during a qualitative research study where we asked respondents, "What does community mean to you?" Many respondents suggested that psychological experiences of community were critical to their working lives. They shared that employers needed to help create conditions that fostered community, and they argued that experiences of community were important to their physical and psychological functioning. They also noted that experiences of community would pay dividends for others at work, for the organization as a whole, and for stakeholders outside of the boundary of the organization. In terms of specific experiences of community, they corroborated the McMillan and Chavis model. Many respondents suggested that *membership* at work was crucial. They needed to feel like they were a part of something, a part of the group, that they belonged. They noted a desire to have *influence*, for their voice to be heard, and that their work mattered. They also expressed a desire for their *needs to be fulfilled*, including basic needs like safe working conditions, and adequate pay to comfortably exist within society, but also their relational needs with coworkers, supervisors, and others across the organization. And, they noted a need for *shared emotional connections*, whether they be in dyads with others or in larger group settings where they could share, vent, laugh, cry, cheer, and engage as social beings. And finally, contrary to any known concepts in the realm of psychological sense of community at that time, they mentioned that experiencing a *sense of community responsibility for others* (i.e., coworkers, the organization, and its stakeholders), without necessarily needing to receive something in return, and potentially risking personal gain, was omnipresent in their conception of community.

These initial observations led to the articulation of the *community experience model* (based primarily on Boyd and Nowell, 2014; Nowell and Boyd, 2014, 2010), which states that psychological community experiences can manifest in two separate forms: (1) the experience of a *community as a resource* and (2) the experience of *community as a responsibility*. We defined these two community experiences and deconstructed their distinct theoretical logics by showing that a sense of community develops when resources are present in the context of an organization that fulfill basic needs and the needs of membership, influence, and shared emotional connection. We also theorized that a sense of community responsibility is created when one's personal values of responsibility toward others intersects with the normative landscape of prosocial responsibility toward others that exists within the context of the organization.

As we proposed (see Figure 1.1), traditional measures of sense of community tend to assess an individual's sense that their community serves as a resource for meeting key psychological and physiological needs (e.g., see the Sense of Community Index [Perkins et al., 1990], the Sense of Community Index-2 [Chavis, Lee, and Acosta, 2008], and the Brief Sense of Community scale [Peterson, Speer, and McMillan, 2008; more to come on measurement systems in Chapter 2]). In other words, we provided theoretical grounding for McMillan and Chavis's (1986) four dimensions as driven by the fulfillment of needs (*membership, influence, integration and fulfillment of needs, and shared emotional connection*), which are especially linked to whether or not an organizational context is serving to meet key psychosocial needs

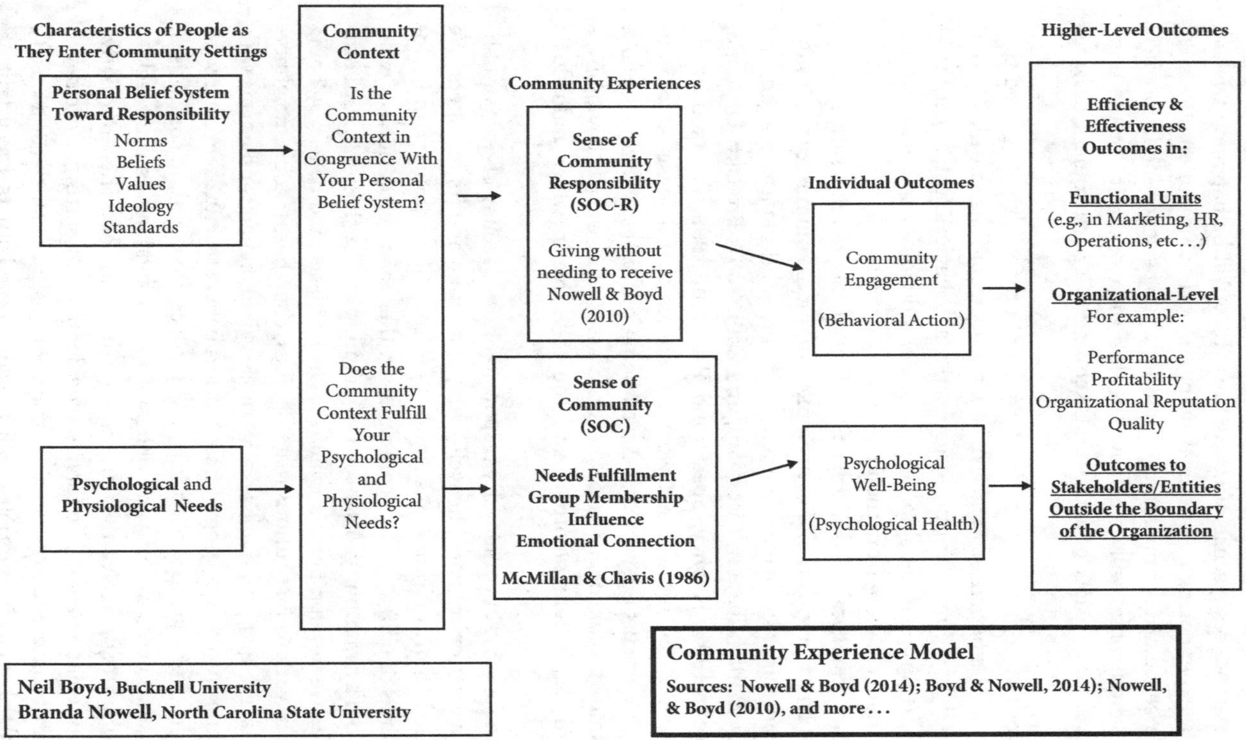

Figure 1.1: The Community Experience Model

A diagram of the community experience model shows how a psychological sense of community and sense of community responsibility develop, and how these constructs impact outcome variables for indivi-duals, work units, organizations, and entities outside the boundary of an organization.

such as the need for affiliation (nAffill), need for power (nPwr), need for achievement (Nach) (McClelland, 1961), and need for affection (Schutz, 1958). The psychological experience of a sense of community was then posited to drive enhanced psychological functioning of the individual. In short, when an employee experiences a sense of community, they will be happier, satisfied, and overall, experiencing a state of thriving at work. Once an employee experiences a sense of community, the community experience model predicts that positive outcomes will be achieved within the work unit, for the organization, and for a variety of external stakeholders (e.g., customers, citizens, clients).

Early work by community psychologists, and others, also suggested that individuals who experienced a sense of community would be more likely to engage in a variety of important pro-organizational behaviors such as organizational citizenship and leadership, and that other individual and organizational outcomes could emanate from their community experiences.

Significant empirical work across a variety of community settings supported this latter proposition. For example, a sense of community was found to predict outcomes like community engagement, political participation, and civic involvement (Albanesi, Cicognani, and Zani, 2007; Brodsky, O'Campo, and Aronson, 1999; Hughey, Speer, and Peterson, 1999; Peterson et al., 2008). However, our more recent work has shown that a sense of community primarily predicts psychological well-being outcomes, whereas a sense of community responsibility is often more associated with behavioral action toward the benefit of others and the collective in which individuals reside.

We define a sense of community responsibility as a feeling of duty or obligation to protect or enhance the well-being of a group and its members. We distinguished from traditional measures of a sense of community in its focus on feelings of obligation to a community rather than perceptions of what one gets from a community. A sense of community responsibility toward others grows as we develop personal values, norms, ideals, and beliefs by being embedded in various institutions (e.g., families, churches, schools, neighborhoods, social groups), and then we carry those values, beliefs, and norms with us as we enter into new settings. These a priori belief structures interact with specific aspects of a given setting (e.g., our work setting) and, in some cases, can evoke sentiments of duty and obligation for individuals as they seek to reconcile who they perceive they are in a given setting and their normative beliefs about what a person like them *should* do in such a setting. Once developed, sense of community responsibility perceptions should increase a variety of prosocial behaviors in one's job, toward coworkers and others, toward the organization as an entity, and toward external stakeholders of the organization (Boyd and Nowell, 2014; Nowell and Boyd, 2014, 2010).

Community Experiences in the Management Literature

In addition to developing theory on community experiences, we explored the application of community experience to workplace settings and attempted to show how community experiences are distinct from similar constructs in the field of management (i.e., organizational commitment, organizational identity, team cohesion, psychological contracts, and social capital; Boyd and Nowell, 2014). From a scientific perspective, showing that a construct is unique is an initial hurdle that must be overcome if one is to begin any detailed investigation into a new concept.[1]

The impetus for this work was created by commentary from management scholars who reviewed our early work and questioned whether or not community experiences were theoretically and methodologically different concepts from well-established constructs in the management literature. They also questioned whether or not community experiences would exhibit better predictive utility on individual and organizational outcomes compared with those same well-regarded factors. The decision to analyze the five management constructs noted earlier was based on an extensive review of the management literature where we searched for other similar relational concepts. We also attempted to find constructs that shared definitional or theoretical commonalities with community experiences. The literature review led us to a belief that these five constructs stand out as ones that are most similar to experiences of community, and the belief that they provide the best litmus test for the utility of community experiences as unique and useful constructs (see Table 1.2).

Team Cohesion. The first related construct is team cohesion. Team cohesion has been described as "the resultant of all the forces which are acting on the members to stay in a group" (Festinger, 1950, p. 274), and "a dynamic process which is reflected in the tendency for a group to stick together and remain united in the pursuit of its goals and objectives" (Carron, 1982, p. 124). In a meta-analytic study, Beal, Cohen, Burke, and McLendon (2003) describe the construct of team cohesion as inclusive of three dimensions: (1) interpersonal attraction, (2) commitment to the task, and (3) group pride. However, community experiences differ from team cohesion in their level of analysis. Team cohesion is specifically an attribute of a team or unit, and community experiences are individual-level constructs that focus on a person's psychological sense of connection to a variety of actors in and around a collective setting. Further, while scholars have examined community experiences in aggregate as a property of a collective, they do not require the assumption of a single "team" or collective task.

1. Portions of this section (including Table 1.2) were previously published in N. Boyd and B. Nowell (2014). Psychological sense of community: A new construct for the field of management. *Journal of Management Inquiry*, *23*(2), 107–122.

Table 1.2 ANALYSIS OF PSYCHOLOGICAL SENSE OF COMMUNITY WITH OTHER CONSTRUCTS

Analysis component	Psychological sense of community (PSOC)	Team cohesion	Organizational identity	Organizational commitment	Psychological contract	Social capital
Definition	A member's feeling of being part of an interdependent community, a feeling that one is part of a larger dependable and stable structure that will meet key needs, and a sense of responsibility for the well-being of that community and its members	The resultant of all the forces that are acting on the members to stay in a group	The degree to which organizational actors have linked his/her organizational membership to his/her self-concept	Staff member's bond of commitment and responsibility to an organization or other organizational target	The perceived obligations that exist between an employer and its employees or the promises an organization is perceived to have made to its employees	A set of resources made available through group members' social relationships
Focus of concept	An individual's cognitive state	A group or task collective	An individual's cognitive state	An individual's cognitive state	An individual's cognitive state	A collective

Dimensions	Membership, Influence, Integration and fulfillment of needs, Shared emotional connection, Sense of responsibility	Interpersonal attraction, Commitment to the task Group pride	Cognitive Emotional	Affective Continuance Normative	Transactional Relational	Structural Relational Cognitive
Level of analysis	Individual	Group or unit	Individual	Individual	Individual	Individual/collective
Referent	Connection to a community of actors	Connection to a team or unit	Connection to an organization	Commitment to a target and restricted to bonds that are sentiments of dedication and responsibility	Connection between an employee and employer	Resources, value, or advantage in a collective
Similarity to PSOC	N/A	Attraction to a group	Affiliation with organization meets key psychological needs for positive identity.	Affective commitment focuses on emotional connection to the organization.	Behavior is driven by perceptions about the relationship between themselves and a context.	Benefits gained via membership

Continued

Table 1.2 *Continued*

Unique to PSOC	N/A	Individual versus group/unit level of analysis PSOC promotes shared: *experience, understanding, and goals.* PSOC focuses on mutual benefits in creating community.	PSOC emphasis on the role of relationships to members as the mechanism for positive identity	PSOC emphasis is specifically targeting a social collective and reflects a range of relational bonds spanning instrumental, commitment, and identification.	PSOC focuses the relationship between the individual and the social context, and not solely on the relationship between employee and employer. PSOC and psychological contracts operationalize different aims. Psychological contracts focus on obligations as a driver of behavior. PSOC is focused on phenomenological experience of a social context as a community.	PSOC focuses on a psychological state whereas social capital centers on resource flow in networks. PSOC focuses on personal perceptions of membership and affiliation.

Organizational Identity. Although a variety of definitions have been proposed, perhaps the most comprehensive definition of organizational identity is (1) feelings of solidarity with the organization, (2) feelings and actions of support for the organization, and (3) perceptions of shared characteristics with other organizational members (Patchen, 1970). As Riketta (2005, p. 361) notes in a fairly recent meta-analysis of the concept, all organizational identity definitions "imply that the organizational member has linked his or her organizational membership to his or her self-concept, either cognitively (e.g., feeling a part of the organization; internalizing organizational values), emotionally (pride in membership), or both."

When comparing organizational identity with community experiences, both constructs reference an individual's cognitive state. They both refer to a sense of membership or connection with the organization that fulfills key needs for a positive identity, but organizational identity is specifically concerned that the individual's values are congruent with the values of the organization. Moreover, while organizational identity focuses on psychological connection to an organization, the specific referent of identification is very broadly defined. Organizations have many facets that may invoke a sense of identification—for example, a staff member may identify with the prestige of the organization, the organization's values, its approach toward satisfying customers, or its leadership. Community experiences are more focused and concerned specifically with the experience inside a human collective.

Organizational Commitment. Organizational commitment was defined by Mowday, Steers, and Porter (1979, p. 226) as the "the relative strength of an individual's identification with and involvement in a particular organization." As one can guess by this definition, researchers treated organizational identity and organizational commitment synonymously for several years (Riketta, 2005). In the late 1980s, researchers in several fields rediscovered organizational identity as a unique construct, and after Ashforth and Mael (1989) outlined the significance of social psychological theories to organizational behavior research, studies on organizational identity as distinct from organizational commitment flourished. In 1990, Allen and Meyer defined three forms of organizational commitment: affective, continuance, and normative, and this three-dimensional framework has emerged as the most prominent model for conceiving organizational commitment (Cohen, 2007).

Specifically, organizational commitment represents a unique type of bond that emphasizes a stance of dedication and responsibility, and it is based on instrumental and normative expectations as well as organizational context. These themes offer clear parallels to the literature on community experiences. Both constructs share a common level of analysis, representing the psychological experience of a relationship by an individual. The literatures of both constructs have recognized that relationships can be rooted in affective, instrumental, and normative bases. For example, sense of community dimensions of membership and shared emotional connection tap into an affective rationale. The dimensions of need fulfillment and influence focus primarily on an instrumental rationale while the dimension of responsibility is based most strongly in a normative rationale.

However, several key distinctions between community experiences and organizational commitment constructs are apparent. Whereas organizational commitment may be associated with a range of referents including a contract or goal (Klein, Molloy, and Brinsfield, 2012), community experiences cannot. Community experiences are not applicable outside of the context of a defined social collective. Second, community experiences and organizational commitment differ in their focal emphasis. For example, Klein et al. (2012) assert that the concept of organizational commitment should be restricted to bonds that are defined by sentiments of dedication and responsibility. Organizational commitment focuses its definitional boundaries on the nature of a bond (i.e., commitment), while being nonspecific on the nature of the target (e.g., Klein et al., 2012). Community experiences seek to be specific on the nature of a target (community) and the content of the bond (e.g., membership and influence) while being inclusive of a range of bond types (e.g., instrumental, commitment, and identification). As such, community experiences are likely a more appropriate construct for investigating organizations as communities, as they seek to capture a more holistic and multidimensional picture of the experience of community.

Psychological Contracts. Psychological contracts refer to the perceived obligations that exist between an employer and its employees (Atkinson, 2007) or the promises an organization is perceived to have made to its employees (Ho, 2005). The literature on psychological contracts has sought to characterize its nature within organizational settings and investigate the outcomes of contract fulfillment and violation or breach on employee attitudes and behavior (Rousseau, 1995; Turnley, Bolino, Lester, and Bloodgood, 2003). The main point of this literature is that the employer/employee relationship is characterized by a number of transactional and relational obligations (Rousseau, 1995). These perceptions are important because the perceived fulfillment or breach of psychological contracts has been shown to have a significant relationship with a number of important employee outcomes such as job satisfaction, intention to stay, and organizational citizenship behavior (e.g., Bal, De Lange, Jansen, and Van Der Velde, 2008; Robinson and Morrison, 1995; Sutton and Griffin, 2004; Turnley and Feldman, 1999, 2000).

The literature on psychological contracts shares common themes with community experiences. Psychological contracts are focused at the individual level of analysis. Both constructs presume an underlying logic that an individual's behavior within a given social context is driven, in part, by their perceptions about the nature of the relationship between themselves and that context. However, psychological contracts involve a very specific relationship within a social context—that between an employee and their employer. Community experiences focus on the perceived relationship of an individual to a social context such as a workplace. Moreover, the literature on psychological contracts focuses on the notion of obligations within a social context and whether perceived obligations are fulfilled or breached as a driver of behavior. Community experiences are focused on the experience of a social context *as a community*.

Social Capital. Oh, Labianca, and Chung (2006) describe social capital as a set of resources made available through group members' social relationships. In their review of the literature on social capital in organizations, they identify four types of resources that can be obtained through social relationships. These include information, political opportunity and influence, emotional support, and mutual trust. However, like organizational commitment, social capital has been subject to a great deal of debate concerning its definition and conceptualization. Adler and Kwon (2002) characterize the diversity of definitions as varying along two dimensions. First, scholars have varied in whether they focus on the substance, sources, or effects of social capital. Second, definitions differ on whether they adopt an individual or collective level of analysis. At the individual level, the focus is on the relations an actor maintains with other actors. At the collective level, the focus is on how the characteristics of relations among a collection of actors facilitate goal accomplishment of the collective.

There are similarities in examining the relationship of organizational social capital and community experiences. Both constructs emphasize benefits that can be gained via membership within a defined social structure. However, the measurement of these two constructs suggests some key points of divergence. First, the level of analysis for community experience is inherently individual. Social capital varies in its application as an attribute to an individual versus an attribute of a collective. However, a collective such as an organization cannot have a high level of community experiences absent of the aggregated level of community experiences of its composite members. Conversely, organizations *can* be theorized to possess social capital that does not necessarily disaggregate to social capital for its individual members. Further, predominant conceptualizations of social capital focus specifically on resources, value, or advantage made possible through networks (Adler and Kwon, 2002; Coleman, 1988; Oh et al., 2006). Different from community experience, social capital is not the perception of advantages made possible through membership; it is the advantage itself and the social structure that confer that advantage. Accordingly, social capital is not a psychological phenomenon but, rather, a sociological phenomenon defined by its function (Coleman, 1988). Consequently, the actual nature and patterns of individual ties among actors in the network are paramount to understanding social capital. These measures are not generally considerations in measures of community experiences. Indeed, it is theoretically possible for an individual to psychologically experience a sense of community with a community of individuals to whom they have relatively limited personal relationships while someone with a great number of personal ties could still feel limited community experience. Even cognitive dimensions of social capital require some measure of consensus or similarity among members and a confirmation that these shared cognitions lead to some individual or collective outcome of value. Measures of community experience require no such reciprocity in cognition.

OK, Community Experiences Are Different: So What?

At this point, I hope that I have convinced you that community experiences are different from other well-regarded concepts in the science of management; however, conceptual clarity and theoretical distinctiveness do not make for a robust form of science. A proper next step was to conduct empirical investigations into the uniqueness of community experience constructs, and their utility in predicting outcomes of importance for individuals within organizations, for the outcomes of the organization, and for stakeholders that are associated with an organization.

As a follow-up to our theoretical work (Boyd and Nowell, 2014; Nowell and Boyd, 2010), a series of empirical studies were conducted in an attempt to determine if a sense of community and a sense of community responsibility would have predictive validity in accordance with propositions in the community experience model. Our first empirical study (Nowell and Boyd, 2014) was conducted in a North Carolina healthcare network organization in which leaders of many healthcare agencies and organizations came together to work on regional state-level healthcare issues and problems. The study had several key findings. First, a sense of community was found to be a unique construct from a sense of community responsibility. Second, consistent with the community experience model, a sense of community was found to be a better predictor of psychological well-being measures (i.e., satisfaction with the group) compared with a sense of community responsibility, and a sense of community responsibility was found to be a better predictor of behavioral engagement (i.e., member leadership action).

A related study by Nowell, Izod, Ngaruiya, and Boyd (2016), also conducted in the North Carolina healthcare collaborative, investigated the intersection and relative contributions of two "other-regarding" motivational constructs in predicting peer nominations of leadership in community collaboratives: public service motivation and psychological sense of community responsibility. Individuals who possess a motivation for public service are thought to seek public service careers where they can give to "others," and once hired in public organizational settings (i.e., nonprofits, NGOs, and public agencies), a public service motivation drives them to be highly psychologically and behaviorally engaged in their work. A key purpose of the study was to introduce a sense of community responsibility to the field of public management as well as clarify the theoretical relationship of public service motivation and sense of community responsibility to each other as well as to indicators of collaborative leadership. The findings indicated that while a sense of community responsibility was significantly related to being identified as stepping up to be a thought leader and a champion of a collaborative, public service motivation had no significant direct relationship to either indicator of collaborative leadership. A major outcome of the study was that a sense of community responsibility became a promising construct for understanding prosocial organizational actions.

Another study by Boyd and Nowell (2017), also conducted in a large healthcare organization, was the first empirical assessment of sense of community and sense of community responsibility within a traditional single organizational setting. The study had multiple aims, including (1) to replicate the previous empirical finding that they were unique constructs, (2) to determine if sense of community was a better predictor of employee well-being compared with a sense of community responsibility, and (3) to determine if a sense of community responsibility was a better predictor of organizational citizenship behavior compared with a sense of community. The findings were remarkably consistent with our collaborative network study (Nowell and Boyd, 2014) in demonstrating that the two concepts are empirically unique. In addition, the data again showed that a sense of community was the best predictor of psychological well-being, and that a sense of community responsibility appeared to consistently predict organizational citizenship better than a sense of community. An additional finding was that, in general, community constructs were better able to predict organizational citizenship behaviors toward individuals (OCBIs) compared with organizational citizenship behaviors toward the organization as a whole (OCBOs). This is an interesting finding and may relate to the fact that the development of a community experience tends to occur within proximal relationships to other individuals at work compared with the entirety of the organization, which is more distal to the action of community development within organizations. For example, performing OCBIs to help coworkers might require the individual to pay attention to coworker needs, provide personal suggestions, engage in direct one-on-one interaction with the coworker, and handle potential resentment that could arise if the helping behavior was ultimately unwanted.

Two newer studies (Boyd and Nowell, 2020; Boyd, Nowell, Zheng, and Hano, 2018) add additional empirical support to the community experience model. The first study (Boyd, Nowell, Zheng, and Hano, 2018) was conducted in a large healthcare organization, and it showed that a sense of community and sense of community responsibility are stronger predictors of psychological well-being and behavioral engagement, respectively, compared with public service motivation. These findings added to the public management literature by showing that community experiences are important direct predictors of public servant outcomes and add to the literature camp that supports the notion that public service motivation is more suited as a predictor of who seeks public service jobs compared with its ability to specifically predict motivation of public servants. The second study (Boyd and Nowell, 2020), conducted in a midsized university, demonstrated that sense of community was the best predictor of psychological well-being (i.e., job satisfaction and thriving) and sense of community responsibility was the best predictor of employee engagement (i.e., organizational citizenship and job engagement) relative to organizational identity, commitment, and public service motivation. These findings are important because they appear to demonstrate that community experiences might be better predictors of employee outcomes compared with constructs in the field of management and public management that have long been revered as important contributors to employee motivation.

Other researchers recently conducted a study with local councilors in a Danish public management setting and demonstrated that leaders with a high level of sense of community responsibility were less likely to retire voluntarily (Pedersen et al., 2020), and consistent with Nowell et al. (2016), a sense of community responsibility was shown to be a strong predictor of visionary leadership behavior. Brincker and Pedersen (2020) also found that a sense of community responsibility acts as a source of job attraction and relocation for East Greenlanders who had been living elsewhere, because they wanted to return home and work as educators to help the youth. In this case, a sense of community with their home region contributed to their sense of community responsibility for others.

The most recent scholarship on community experiences has revolved around factors that can help managers and leaders to build communities in organizations. For example, Livne-Tarandach and Jazaieri (2021) showed how a swift sense of community can be cultivated within a collective in as few as 5 days. Their work showed that brief supportive connections that were made durable by resourcing artifacts that created scaffolds that mobilize actors to create a web of connections led to an organization-wide swift sense of community. Jonsen, Boyd, Oikelome, and Trimble (2022) showed that experiences of community can be incorporated by human resource management professionals who are interested in developing high-involvement work climates.

Finally, the work of Boyd and Larson (2023a) in a large healthcare system showed that a series of antecedent factors can drive or hinder the development of community experiences. Their work showed that organizational size, hierarchy, geographical dispersion, excessive centralization and standardization, a hyperfocus on cost containment and efficiency, and frequent leadership transitions all hinder development of community at work. They further showed that the C-suite plays a key role in promoting, messaging, and implementing interventions toward community at work, and that experiences of community are most likely generated by characteristics of connectivity within work units. Results also demonstrated that individual employee characteristics of empathy, optimism, and caring matter in the creation of community, and that ego and self-centered individuals erode community experiences. Such characteristics in managers had cascading impacts on employees, as many respondents felt that unit managers were the linchpin in creating community contexts at work, and that the work unit was the most important epicenter for community development. Their findings showed that HR professionals play important roles by building community constructs into job analysis, job descriptions, recruiting, hiring, training, performance appraisal, and the myriad systems of HR. Such actions were thought to be important interventions that would institutionalize a focus on community at work within the DNA of the organization.

A follow-up study (Boyd and Larson, 2023b) in the same organization showed that clan cultures (Cameron and Quinn, 1999) are important cultural antecedents to community experiences. The clan culture organization is bound together by loyalty and tradition. The working environment is friendly, people have a lot in common, and it feels like a family. Teamwork, participation, and consensus are valued, and leaders act as mentors. Success is defined by addressing the needs of clients and caring for people. This latest work will be highlighted as the primary objective of Chapter 4, in which we discuss how to design and build communities at work.

Final Thoughts and Implications for Amanda

At their core, organizations are collectives, comprised of individuals who participate in coordinated action. While workplaces differ in important ways from geographic communities such as neighborhoods, towns, and regions, they also share many similarities. Individuals seek membership into these collectives for a variety of reasons, including the desire to obtain resources, gain influence, attain a sense of belonging and affiliation, find and develop positive relationships with others, and engage in responsible stewardship of the collective. As such, the metaphor of community applies to organizations as much as it does to neighborhoods or towns.

In this chapter, we introduced the community experience framework and showed how it has utility in organizational settings and other domains of inquiry. In the field of community psychology, a sense of community has been a fruitful construct for explaining important outcomes such as citizen participation, residence, psychological health and well-being, and voluntary engagement in community betterment efforts in neighborhoods and schools. New research has discovered the importance of a sense of community responsibility, and how it may drive a variety of behavioral actions within organizations. Community experiences have the potential to impact outcomes such as organizational citizenship behavior, staff retention, and employee wellness, and these types of issues should be of concern to both practitioners and scholars. This work echoes the calls of management authors like Mintzberg (2009), Block (2008), and others who believe that community building is the next major domain of development for leaders and managers, and those who believe that developing a sense of community and a sense of community responsibility are important endeavors at work.

A question in Amanda's journey is whether or not she has the knowledge, skills, and abilities to conceive, design, and build community at work. Her educational background, management worldviews, and current skills may be at odds with such an understanding and capability. And, while aspects of family life with Ken, Gabby, and Jensen seem wonderful, there are some hints that the balancing act of work and home life is challenging to say the least. In this chapter, you were exposed to new ideas and research findings that Amanda may not yet know, and we can wonder if the acquisition of that knowledge alone is what Amanda will need to catapult her on a trajectory of enlightenment and action. Or, perhaps we will find that the ability to understand and build community at work is more complex than merely understanding the academic literature that we have encountered so far. In my opinion, Amanda's journey is a common one in organizations today, and one that might resonate with you. There are things she will need to learn and experience before she is fully ready to embrace and behaviorally help her organization on a path toward building a culture of community. And, we can also wonder if that educational path might have implications for a greater sense of community and responsibility at home and in other collectives that she inhabits.

CHAPTER 2

Life Is Great and the Community Imperative

LIFE IS GREAT

In many ways, Amanda was very fortunate. She grew up in an upper-middle class family with a father who was an advertising executive for a large agency, and a mother who doted over the three children and worked part-time jobs to help financially sustain the family. She never wanted for anything substantial, and her privilege allowed her to explore areas of passion. The freedom she had led her to art and design school, and she remembers how proud she was that she could live her dream of being whatever she wanted. She was talented. She honed her design skills and won two major competitions while in school. The second, the prestigious Walker Award for Fashion Innovation and Design, was a national award that provided an opportunity to show her work at the famed fashion week in New York City. And that day proved to be the first catalyst of many that moved her career to the fast lane. She recounted the event in a *New York Times* fashion article last year by stating, "Meeting Dan that night changed everything."

Dan, a successful venture capitalist, philanthropist of the arts, and shrewd businessman who liked to help others, while helping his financial portfolio, changed the game for Amanda. After the show, he approached her backstage, and after exchanging a series of pleasantries and commentaries of how much he loved her work, he said, "We should talk." Within weeks, those talks led to a million-dollar investment that gave Dan a 20% stake in Amanda's company, with her retaining operational control of the firm, and Dan taking a silent partner role in the shadows. The relationship proved to be a success, and it led to a line of fashion-forward tops for women that sold like hotcakes. The revenues from that venture allowed for incremental growth in office

Building Community at Work. Neil Boyd, Oxford University Press. © Oxford University Press (2025).
DOI: 10.1093/9780197635964.003.0003

staff in sales and promotions, slack resources to get the balance sheet in order, and opportunities to invest in the next apparel rollouts. The first three launches were wildly successful, but then came the fourth, an accessories line of scarves, hats, and belts that for some reason didn't gain the traction she wanted. It wasn't a total loss, but after the sell-off late in the season, they weren't able to break even. Amanda took it hard. She didn't like losing, and, more importantly, she didn't like being wrong. She had been sure the accessories line would be successful, but she rolled with the punches and remembered her investments professor's wise words from several years earlier when he exclaimed, "A diversified mix of instruments will not always yield winners. In fact, that's the point of diversification, to create a balanced portfolio that can stand the test of time." It has been a year since the divestment of the accessories line, but that experience still resonates in Amanda's mind.

She arrived at the board meeting at 7:55 a.m., grabbed a third cup of coffee, and sat down at the conference table. "Good morning," she exclaimed to Sarah, the director of HR, and Juan, the director of marketing and social media, who had arrived earlier. Within minutes, several others joined the room, and Jim, the chair of the finance and budget committee, phoned in via conference call. "So how are we doing?" Amanda said. Linda, the chief financial officer (CFO), chimed in and said,

> Well, quarterly profits are up 1.3% in the same period compared to recent past years, and we had a successful launch of a new trouser line this past month. We were smart to outsource production of that line to Vietnam because we are saving an additional 20% per employee, in full-time equivalents (FTEs), compared to our previous vendor. Sarah, you did a great job helping us find qualified outsourcing via your labor market analysis.

Linda continued on for the next 10 minutes with various updates, at which point Amanda asked, "So Jim, what do you think about what Linda is sharing?" "I like it," Jim said. "I like what I'm hearing about our current earnings per share (EPS) and projections forward, the return on investment (ROI) data on recent capital expenditures looks good, and I love how we're driving down labor costs via overseas vendors." After a lengthy exchange between Jim and others on the financial picture of the firm, Juan presented an update on marketing efforts:

> Our new Instagram platform is doing well as likes and mentions are up by a combined 18% from last month, and our Google Analytics are showing that web hits are steady and aligned with our recent strategy. I'm especially happy with how the click data correlate with the new trouser line sales, and it's pretty clear that

> our investments in Facebook posting are generating website traffic to targeted products that we are trying to push. All in all, things are moving along nicely.

Amanda was happy to hear that across the board sales were either steady or growing because her goal for this year was to continue to grow the business at a modest pace, which would allow for expansion and greater diversification of the product and service mix in the coming year.

The meeting was about to end, but Amanda casually asked, "So anything else folks?" Everyone looked around the table without much of an utterance, but just before they were about to pack up and leave, Sarah said,

> Well, I'm not sure how to say this, but I've heard some rumblings about our work culture from a few managers. Apparently, it's been going on for a while, but I'm not sure what to make of it. It seems like some of the employees are feeling overworked and underappreciated.

"Hmmmmm, OK," Amanda said. "I'm not sure about that either. Honestly, I'm very surprised to hear that. We pay above-market wages, comply with all of the employment laws that are on the books, and provide competitive healthcare and retirement benefits. What else could they want?" "I don't know," Sarah said. "I'll look into it." And with that, the meeting was adjourned.

THE COMMUNITY IMPERATIVE

Amanda is experiencing a situation about the culture of her organization that she isn't ready to handle. She is surprised that the employees are grumbling, and everything she has been taught or experienced to date hasn't prepared her to have immediate solutions to the problem. A big question for you to consider is "Why is she surprised?" My guess is that you have some immediate answers based on your experiences and after reading Chapter 1, but I also believe that the question has a complex array of potential responses.

Being surprised in a work situation usually means that you have not experienced the event before, and therefore you don't have anything from your past behavior to grab onto, or it could mean that you haven't been intellectually exposed to the situation in school or in training and development sessions. I think that Amanda, like so many others in leadership and management today, are apt to be in this situation as it relates to community at work. The more one is exposed to management situations that require problem-solving, the more one becomes proficient in producing appropriate solutions. Management practice over time can certainly lead to growth and improvement of one's capabilities; however, I also believe that there are a series of underlying conditions that are acting as gatekeepers to Amanda's thinking.

Let's start first with education. Amanda is a high school graduate, a graduate of one of the finest fashion and design institutes in the United States, and she earned an MBA with a specialization in accounting and finance. You have to wonder where in all of those years of education she was exposed to concepts, models, and theories of organizational culture, and many of its subthemes, including the concept of community. Based on your reading so far, you can surmise that she probably wasn't exposed to the concept of community at work during any of her degrees, and it is highly doubtful that she has ever met a community psychologist or read anything from the community psychology literature. The study of community in organizations is so new that the vast majority of practicing managers and leaders in today's organization have never been exposed to the concept of community and the psychological constructs of a sense of community or sense of community responsibility. In fact, because you read Chapter 1, you probably already know more about community at work than the vast majority of individuals in the world. However, Amanda must have been exposed to the study of organizational culture and employee issues during her MBA, right?

The current state of MBA and business undergraduate education is rooted in a long history that has shaped what students learn, and the lenses through which they view the world. The first business degrees were designed to be a mirror reflection of the way corporations were structured. In the language of Michael Porter's (1985) value chain logic, corporations have a main business process (e.g., they make products or they design services), and they have support functions that align to, and "support," the main business process. In terms of organizational structure, a corporation that has grown large enough to require specialization in various areas will at some point become a functional organization. A functional organization has "functional units," which carry out various specializations, and when business degrees were first designed, the functional organization included units like accounting, finance, marketing, personnel (now HR), operations, and others. Thus, business programs almost always had a core program where students would take at least one course in each of the major functional unit areas. They most likely would also take a core course in macro- and/or microeconomics. Almost 70 years have passed since the great expansion of business programs in universities, and not much has changed. Most undergraduate business degrees still orient to the functional organization structure, and MBA programs are commonly structured the same way. Instead of one course in a functional area, MBA students are commonly exposed to two (or more) courses in various functional areas. In Amanda's case, she was likely exposed to one course in each of the major functional areas and then completed several specialty courses in accounting and finance.

At most, like so many others, she completed one course in human resource management.

The state of human resource management education is also intriguing. HR professionals typically have three major charges in their jobs: (1) to execute the instrumental functions of HR; (2) to design, implement, and store personnel files and records; and (3) to advocate for the needs of employees. The first two charges, and especially the first objective, is how human resource courses and programs are designed. An introductory HR course most often contains topics in job analysis, recruiting, hiring, training and development, performance appraisal, compensation and benefits, and labor relations. And, after an introductory course, HR students typically complete specific courses in each (or most) of the instrumental areas noted above. I use the term *instrumental* here to indicate that students often learn how to execute a particular task toward the achievement of a particular objective. For example, when students learn how to design hiring systems, they often learn how to create a résumé (biodata), how to interview, and other hiring methods that will lead to predictions of future work performance in the name of effectiveness and efficiency. At a sophisticated level, organizations will conduct concurrent and/or predictive validity studies to show that their hiring methods can forecast future employee performance and other key criteria of interest. Note that the most common criterion of interest is performance, and that it is the most typical instrumental goal that serves the interests of the organization. Performance is merely one goal of a holistic person, and yet HR techniques like hiring and others are often designed to serve specific interests of the organization. By default, HR students are commonly trained to carry out the instrumental wishes of the executive team that resides in the corporate suite (C-suite), and even if they are interested in being advocates for their employees, that task is often relegated to a back burner in favor of instrumental execution.

At the very most, Amanda and other business students are exposed to the topic of organizational culture in a single chapter of a human resource management course (e.g., in an employee relations chapter), or if offered as part of the core curriculum program, they might take a course in organizational behavior. Organizational behavior is the study of people in organizations and typically includes topics like leadership, motivation, teams and group dynamics, power, negotiation, and others. It is possible that a chapter on organizational culture is included in an organizational behavior class, but of course, that would be at the discretion of the professor. And, even if students learned about organizational culture, their exposure would usually be fairly superficial. Because Amanda completed a focus in accounting and finance in her MBA program, it is extremely unlikely that she had any exposure to organizational culture and how to design and create a culture that employees would describe as fulfilling and helping them lead a life of purpose and thriving.

Her education, and the education of so many business students over the years, has been significantly shaped by the mirroring of curricula to the structure and functions within corporations. Lectures, cases, assignments, and other pedagogical tools are often centered on learning how to make an organization financially viable. Business education too often focuses on teaching strategies of growth, revenue generation, strong profit and loss statements, excellent financial marginal analysis, and competing to win. And, because of its instrumental orientation, students are commonly taught *how* to do things but not necessarily taught as much on *why* we should do it a certain way, and how to critique the status quo methods of our time. Of course, there are a variety of excellent business programs that include critical thinking and critical theorizing toward the discipline of business and management, but a critical lens is less common historically.

As a contrast to such an orientation, I work in a college of management that, on the one hand, still holds on to vestiges of the past in its structure and philosophy but, on the other hand, is influenced by faculty members and others who believe that a college of management is different from a college of business. An "M-school" is different from a "B-school" in that it can be designed as a values-driven enterprise instead of an instrumentally driven organization. This means bringing topics of ethics, justice, and critical theory to the foreground, and integrating interdisciplinary perspectives from diverse fields across the university in management courses or in syncopation with such offerings. In addition, an M-school can help students understand that organizations are purpose driven. In other words, every organization should be conceived through the lens of providing critical or important products, services, or programs that are needed in our world, and that satisfy important needs that serve the common good in addition to the self-interests of owners and leaders. Within this orientation, an M-school can be designed to expose students to a variety of organizational forms in the private, nonprofit, and public sector, instead of a heavy dose of private sector education, which dominates business school education even today.

An M-school can be designed to help students understand the most pressing problems on the globe (i.e., wicked problems or grand challenges), like climate change, social inequities, and poverty. In short, a program can be designed to bring social, environmental, and economic justice to the foreground and deliver that content in concert (or in opposition) to the notions of economic growth and shareholder value. And, an M-school can be designed with a focus on people as opposed to a focus on the instrumental activities of the firm as an entity that takes center stage.

For example, I teach an undergraduate course to first- and second-year students where they design and run a social entrepreneurship company. The mission of their organization must align to one or more of the 17 United

Nations (UN) Sustainable Development Goals (see https://sdgs.un.org/goals), and their primary mission is to deliver services to a local community organization. They also have a co-mission to design and sell a product that produces revenue to support the social mission of the organization. In addition, students are taught that organizations have three major components: Effectiveness, Efficiency, and Community, and they are expected to design, perform, and reflect on each of these components in everything they do. The students are taught how to design socially conscious services and products, they analyze value chain activity (their service and business core activities and all support activities in the organization) from a triple-bottom-line lens (people, planet, prosperity), and they actively experience how community intersects with everything they do. They elect their leadership where students prepare speeches and "run" for various senior leadership roles, including chief executive officer (CEO), vice president of accounting and finance, vice president of communications, vice presidents of business and service, and a vice president of HR. During the elections, students are encouraged to align their votes for candidates by analyzing how they might deliver effectiveness, efficiency, and community. Moreover, once the VP of HR has been elected, they design and run a job fair for the remaining employees of the company for job assignments, and job descriptions are encouraged to include language about community. Within the HR unit, the company often creates a position called the "quality of work-life manager," and this person designs measurement systems and reports out during the semester on how the company is functioning as a community. If Amanda had taken a course like this, she would have been required to confront organizational culture and community at work through conceptual models, measurement instruments, and problem-solving methods to build community in organizations. Moreover, the visceral experience of learning about community in action would have been an invaluable experience because it would have helped her to be prepared as issues of culture and community arose in her future personal and work life.

You might ask: So how was such an amazing course created? Well, it was the initial invention of John Miller in 1979, a management professor at Bucknell University, who believed that an introductory management course should be designed with a "learning by doing" philosophy instead of trying to teach students from a textbook who had essentially no experience in management settings (Miller, 1991). John was also interested in integrating organizational behavior concepts, models, and theories into the course, which allowed students to engage in deep reflection and introspection about their thoughts and actions in relation to other individuals and groups in the company. When Tammy Hiller joined the course in the 1990s, with a Ph.D. in organizational behavior (remember, that's the field of management that studies humans in organizations), she stimulated an enhanced focus on integrating social justice elements into the course. Jamie Hendry (who is a strong proponent of environmental justice and other justice causes too) and Eric Martin (who is committed to justice and common-good causes) significantly influenced the course, and when I joined the class in 2013, we collectively solidified mission connections to the UN Sustainable Development Goals, and other social justice/sustainability elements throughout the course. Further, community was already an important introspective construct in the course before I arrived at Bucknell, but I helped to expose students to the community experience model as a way to guide attempts at building community in their companies (see Hendry, Hiller, Martin, and Boyd, 2017, for a full review of the evolution of the course). You can see that it was the influence of people who championed justice and sustainability, and my personal background and knowledge in community psychology, that helped to create an educational environment that allows Bucknell students to read, understand, and practice the execution of building community in a company early in their academic careers.

Another underlying condition in business schools, which is influenced by formal education, but also a pervasive narrative in our society, is a hyperfocus on accounting and financial constructs as the main driver of the organization. You can already see how higher education degrees in business play a role in this, but remember, business education was designed to mirror the corporate world. And, the narrative of "profits over people," has been with us for a very long time. As Milton Friedman (1970) once proclaimed, the only social responsibility of the firm is to its shareholders. Friedman's claim was mostly directed toward social and environmental causes outside the boundary of the firm, but one can easily conceive that a hyperfocus on shareholders creates blinders that gatekeep attention toward other critical stakeholders in and around organizations. For sure, employees have been regarded as important stakeholders for as long as collective action was needed to pursue organizational goals, but more importantly, many leaders and managers aren't equipped with the cognitive tools to understand and build community at work.

A hyperfocus on profit and other organizational outcomes that serve shareholders creates organizational contexts that become a self-fulfilling prophecy in chasing those goals. We see this narrative played out in boards of directors that have an abundance of individuals who subscribe to this narrative, and we have certainly seen the manifestation of this narrative within the C-suite of most corporations across the globe. Of course, things are changing, but it is still common today to see C-suite structure where the CEO and CFO are attached at the hip. CEO and CFO offices are often in close proximity to each other so that these two critical minds can plan how to run the organization. Further, the vast majority of CEOs in the last century have risen to the CEO rank via previously holding the CFO role. And, this action alone is very much responsible for the transfer of the narrative that profits matter over people.

It is much less likely that a VP of marketing or a VP of HR has ascended, or will ascend, to the CEO position, and you may not know that in the field of HR, one of the recent presidents of the Society of Human Resource Management (SHRM) exclaimed that "we [finally] have a seat at the table." This comment is enlightening because as the field of personnel transitioned to HR in the past several decades, HR professionals did not have an equal seat at the C-suite table. And, for the longest time, they were trying to gain that seat at the table and become an equal partner in running the organization. The SHRM president was announcing, to HR professionals, by the way, that they had made it. That they had finally gained an equal seat in contributing to strategic human resource management means that they are now being regarded as involved in the strategic direction of the firm with other members of the C-suite. However, this change in the stature of HR is so new that neither Amanda nor most of the members of C-suites across the world would have any idea about this change. Perhaps Sarah, her VP of HR, would have manifested this idea to others on the leadership team, but to do so would be to challenge a dominant pervasive narrative of our society, which would take some work. It certainly would require much more work than merely continuing with status quo thinking that money drives everything in organizations. Money is important, and it is a key energic input to any organization, but a hyperfocus on it can limit our ability to see other important things that must gain attention.

We should also be clear to state that the CEO–CFO alignment issue, and the narrative of "the bottom line," extends throughout the C-suite in ways that influence immediate reactions to the problem of community at work. The most skilled person in the room, who should have most of the answers toward the problem, is the VP of HR. However, remember what I said about the instrumental nature of HR education. The response of an HR professional toward community at work is likely to be more sophisticated than Amanda's, but it also has a likelihood to be instrumental in its orientation. For example, when employee problems arise, it is common for leaders and managers (and even HR professionals), to wonder if the problem can be fixed with more pay, better benefits, improved training, and other interventions that neatly fit within instrumental domains of HR education and practice. As you will learn in future chapters, an appropriate response to the problem of community at work is much more nuanced, sophisticated, and demanding of particular skill sets that are not commonly present in the majority of C-suites today. It requires humancentric approaches and investments into activities that are not ordinarily perceived to be worth the expenditures. It requires conceptual lenses that are not commonly understood, and it requires tools that are not frequently learned and experienced by leaders and managers. And, at its core, it requires an approach to the whole person instead of a mindset that orients to the transactional nature of an employment contract, which states, "you work and we pay you."

Remember in Chapter 1 when I introduced you to the concept of psychological contracts (Rousseau, 1995), which is the perceived obligation that exists between an employer and employees (Atkinson, 2007), or the promises an organization is perceived to have made to its employees (Ho, 2005)? The transactional nature of an employment contract is an exceptionally limited view toward a psychological contract, which, in contrast, includes all of the perceived obligations that an employer promised. An expanded psychological contract involves employer obligations that basic, safety, social, and even aspirational goals like self-actualization can be achieved (Maslow, 1943, 1987). On the employee side of an expanded psychological contract, they are expected to show up to work, work productively and efficiently, and in general, contribute to the well-being of people, their work unit, the organization, and its stakeholders. A problem arises when the logic of an expanded psychological contract interacts with an organizational culture that supports a "profit over people" narrative and a setting where limited transactional employment contracts are normed. When these conditions are present, employees experience increased psychological contract violations, and significant acute violations, or the accumulation of violations, will predict reductions in job satisfaction, intention to stay, and organizational citizenship behavior (e.g., Bal, De Lange, Jansen, and Van Der Velde, 2008; Robinson and Morrison, 1995; Sutton and Griffin, 2004; Turnley and Feldman, 1999, 2000). In short, a high level of psychological contract violations in a workplace will breed a setting where people are unhappy, unfulfilled, unproductive, and as Gareth Morgan (1986) noted, "stuck in a psychic prison." Such a workplace is the anthesis of a thriving community, especially a community that is grounded in the psychological experiences of community, and leaders and managers have an obligation to design organizational cultures that avoid and reduce both the acute and accumulative development of psychological contract violations.

Whether or not you would describe your current work environment as a psychic prison is an individually based perception, but even if you wouldn't go to that descriptive extreme, all of us have experienced either acute or accumulative psychological contract violations. Their existence and pervasiveness in organizations are certainly related to the fact that most workers today are unhappy in their jobs. A recent comprehensive study conducted jointly by the Lumina Foundation, the Bill & Melinda Gates Foundation, Omidyar Network, and Gallup showed that less than 50% of US workers were satisfied at work (Kelly, 2019). Gallup has been measuring employee engagement in the United States since 2000, and they found that less than one-third of US workers are engaged in their jobs, and 17.5% are actively disengaged, which means that they resent their jobs, complain to coworkers, and actively demonstrate low morale. In total, Gallup reports that 68.5% of American workers aren't happy at work (Wilke, 2017).

These studies showed that a variety of factors are at play, including poor working conditions in jobs, spending too much time at work, stagnant pay, pay inequity, fewer promotion opportunities, increased healthcare costs, and fewer benefits for employees, yet workers were more likely to report that they were holding a good job when they were allowed to create, were allowed to learn new skills, and were encouraged to focus on quality over quantity. The findings showed that disengagement correlated with a variety of behavioral reactions on the job, including drinking alcohol (5%), taking naps (15%), checking or posting on social media (60%), shopping online (55%), playing pranks on coworkers (40%), and watching Netflix (11%). The suggested managerial and leadership "fixes" for employee dissatisfaction and engagement were telling. As we would expect, the most common solutions to this problem included instrumental actions like better pay and benefits, increased opportunities for advancement, access to better kinds of work, and several suggestions that focused on coping mechanisms for workers like getting better sleep, relaxation techniques, and developing more resilience in the face of stressors.

I find this latter narrative akin to "blaming the victim," and it is very out of touch with the reality of why workers feel unhappy and disengaged at work. Consistent with the community experience model, employees require basic needs to be fulfilled (i.e., adequate pay, benefits, working conditions, time off, safety, etc.), which is like taking care of one's basic hygiene. Leaders who do not fulfill these types of needs are egregiously and acutely breaking their psychological contract with employees. Moreover, employees have higher order affiliative needs, including a desire for respect, trust, acceptance, belonging, social engagement, and mattering. A workplace that ignores these higher order needs is also actively contributing to psychological violations, and as I have stated before, managers and leaders are not as readily equipped to provide solutions to these sorts of problems. Instead, they often blame the victim and suggest that employees need to develop better attitudes, and they sometimes opine that workers should stop complaining and be happy they have a job. Of course, merely having a job is not enough for individuals to thrive and feel that they are living a purpose-driven life.

As you can see, the transactional employment contract narrative has stimulated generations of leaders and managers to focus on a very narrow set of instrumental responsibilities to solve the problem of unhappy and disengaged workers. Instead, we need a new way of thinking and action that creates a path forward where leaders know how to build thriving communities at work. Unfortunately, recent evidence suggests that workers are striking at concerning rates (Kallas, Ritchie, and Friedman, 2022), which is an indication that people are fed up because their basic resource and affiliative needs are not being met. For example, from 2021 to 2022, the total number of work stoppages increased by 52% (279 to 424) and the total number of workers on strike increased by 60% (~140,000 to ~224,000). Workers in the accommodation and food services industry organized the greatest number of work stoppages, and the majority of all workers involved in work stoppages came from the educational services industry (~135,380, or roughly 60%). These are hardly numbers that indicate thriving communities at work.

Beyond the depressing statistics and commentary that I have offered here, I also believe that we are in the midst of an inflection point regarding public discourse and action around social justice issues that permeate across organizational boundaries. Recent social movements have highlighted new narratives around Black lives, LGBTQ+ rights, marijuana legalization and decriminalization, Indigenous rights, climate change, criminal justice reform, #MeToo, new populism, and the staggering market share of wealth of the 1%. And, it is clear that community psychologists (among a variety of academic disciplines) have been significantly contributing to these areas of scholarship (e.g., *criminal justice*—Schuck, 2020; *Indigenous communities*—Ciofalo, Dudgeon, and Nikora, 2022; *microaggressions*—Bond and Haynes-Baratz, 2022; Costa et al., 2023; *LBGTQ+*—Moran, Chen, and Tryon, 2018; *racism*—Collins et al., 2023; *sustainability*—Harré, Blythe, McLean, and Khan, 2022). The presence of such social discourse has been challenged by political leaders across the globe and has created more divisiveness than most of us can remember in our entire lives. Yet, the presence of these social movements also means that people are fed up with the status quo, and they are seeking a future that promotes individual autonomy, justice, and a focus on the common good. These movements also highlight that people seek a life where they are accepted, valued, and are given dignity by others. The past decade shows that, unfortunately, we have a long way to go in the fight for a world, and a working world, where such goals are to be achieved and normalized. Yet, at the same time, we also see a shift in how these social movements have stimulated discourse and action in organizations.

One of the biggest signals that social movement discourse has infused corporate thinking is the escalating desire to focus on diversity, equity, and inclusion (DEI). Corporations are hiring DEI leaders and staffing their divisions, they are taking a public stance on DEI and other social justice issues, and they are providing opportunities for employees at all organizational levels to discuss, plan, and change the state of the status quo. Organizations across sectors are increasing a DEI presence on their websites and in their practices through imagery, language, reports, committees, and personnel embodiment, and by altering their vision and value statements to reflect that they desire to create organizations where everyone is included and matters.

The academic literature is burgeoning with descriptive, theoretical, and empirical papers on DEI topics. Community psychologists have added to this debate with some interesting and nuanced work. For example, Neal and Neal (2013) noted that recent theoretical and empirical work has uncovered a community–diversity dialectic where factors that foster diversity often run in opposition to those that create a sense of community. They argue that it might not be possible to create collectives that simultaneously foster respect for diversity and a sense of community. Stivala, Robins, Kashima, and Kirley (2016) examined the (in)compatibility of diversity and sense of community, and they found that diversity and highly clustered social networks are incompatible when diversity features of the individual are easily observable or "embodied"; however, the incompatibility breaks down when cultural diversity is sufficiently large. In other words, segregation based on immutable characteristics such as race can possibly be overcome by sufficient similarity on mutable characteristics based on cultures where the scope of cultural possibilities and social influence processes are more diffuse.

Further, a recent publication by Bond and Haynes-Baratz (2022) addressed microaggressions toward individuals from marginalized groups within the workplace. They noted that harmful microaggressions pervade organizations, which requires an urgent and immediate need for leaders to implement strategies to foster equitable and inclusive work environments. They propose a bystander-focused approach to address microaggressions with the "Get a (Collective) GRIP" framework. The framework emphasizes that active bystanders employ an ecological scan that includes *a*ssessing what happened, determining one's *g*oals for intervening, considering the *r*elationships among those involved in the incident (target/s, transgressor/s, and witness/es), taking into account the *i*nstitutional context in which the incident occurs, and being attuned to structural issues and *p*ower dynamics within the context. As dialogues about DEI continue to evolve, the community psychology literature is clearly a logical place for scholars and practitioners to enhance their understanding on how to conceive and enact appropriate DEI policies and actions in organizations.

The literature is also significantly expanding on a variety of topics in the realm of social, environmental, and economic justice. There is a strong argument to be made that the academic and practical disciplines of management, human resource management, and organizational behavior are in the midst of a revolution. The "old-school" mentality emphasizing profits at all costs is shifting to a new world order of thinking where financial exigencies are considered in direct conjunction with environmental and social issues. Academics have been studying corporate social responsibility, and concepts like triple-bottom-line management, and practicing managers have been engraining multiple-bottom-line decision-making into the daily routines of employees throughout the system of individual firms, and across the networks of interconnected organizations. Environmental, social, and governance reporting (ESG; formerly called corporate social responsibility reporting) is continuing to evolve in ways that more fully account for environmental and social justice measures. Early adopters of corporate social responsibility reporting often used the UN Global Compact as a guide to measure the triple bottom line. Launched in 2000 by former UN Secretary-General Kofi Annan, the UN Global Compact was initiated to bring business and the UN together to give a human face to the global market (https://unglobalcompact.org).

The UN Compact was comprised of 10 principles across the categories of human rights, labor, environment, and anticorruption, and companies did their best to report corporate activity to the principles. Within a few years, however, the Global Reporting Initiative (GRI) appeared to become the "standard" reporting method because it provided a much more detailed rubric for evaluation of economic, environmental, social, and governance activities, and it allowed for better comparison between organizations (www.globalreporting.org). The first version of what was then the GRI Guidelines (G1) was published in 2000, and as demand for GRI reporting and uptake from organizations steadily grew, the guidelines were expanded and improved, leading to G3 (2006) and G4 (2013). In 2016, GRI transitioned from providing guidelines to setting the first global standards for sustainability reporting—the GRI Standards. The Standards continue to be updated and added to, including new Standards on Tax (2019) and Waste (2020), a major update to the Universal Standards (2021), and the continued rollout of Sector Standards (2022).

In recent years, in addition to GRI reporting, many companies are now indexing off of the Sustainability Accounting Standards Board (SASB) standards (www.sasb.org), and the UN Sustainable Development Goals (sdgs.un.org/goals). There has also been a strong corporate entity movement to create a new incorporated organizational form called a Benefit Corporation, which at the time of this writing, is a legal organizational form in 35 states and the District of Columbia (DC). A benefit corporation is a legal entity that is chartered to intentionally direct portions of profit to social, environmental, and/or economic justice causes. In addition, B-Lab, which was formed in Berwyn, Pennsylvania, in 2006 as an organization to conduct B-Corp Certification, has grown substantially over the past 15+ years (https://www.bcorporation.net). In 2007, they certified 82 organizations, and in their 2021 annual report, cofounders Andrew Kassoy and Bart Houlahan stated the following:

> In 2021, the global community of Certified B Corporations grew to a total of +4,300 businesses in 77 countries. Over the course of 2020–2021, 6,000 applications for certification came in from around the globe, and 50,000 new companies registered to use the B Impact Assessment to understand how they measure up to high environmental and social standards—a nearly 40% increase over the previous two years. And it's not just more B Corps, but bigger B Corps: 30 public companies are now certified, 15 of which had their IPOs [Initial Public Offering] in the last year—reflecting the growing conversation in the financial sector around stakeholder governance.

This new way of thinking has not been lost on nonprofits, NGOs, and governmental organizations, as they too have been moving in a direction toward a sustainable future (Adams, Muir, and Hoque, 2014; Portney, 2013). The sustainability revolution has stimulated the development of new theories, models, and concepts that are shaping practical applications in organizational settings. And, while many of the advances have come in the area of environmental sustainability, new innovations are developing in relation to social bottom-line issues. As it directly relates to human experiences at work, the fields of human resource management, organizational behavior, and a variety of others are experiencing significant growth on topics that relate to the human condition at work. By way of example, a psychological concept that has gained traction across multiple disciplines is *thriving at work*. As Spreitzer et al. (2005) note, thriving at work is the joint experience of learning and vitality, where a worker is able to grow, develop, and feel energized. Vitality is an energized state, where employees feel passion and excitement for their work. Vitality can also be contagious and spread to others who are proximate to the employee. Learning is the acquisition of knowledge and skills that help an employee achieve desired personal and professional goals. As an employee is able to learn new things and develop as a whole person these conditions feed their vitality. Moreover, employees who are energized with a sense of vitality can see it dissipate without opportunities to grow and develop. In addition, thriving has been theoretically distinguished by psychologists and others to related concepts like resilience (Carver, 1998; Masten and Reed, 2002; Sutcliffe and Vogus, 2003), flourishing (Keyes and Haidt, 2003), subjective well-being (Diener et al., 1999), flow (Csikszentmihalyi, 1990), and self-actualization (Maslow, 1998). Workers who are thriving are truly *living* in organizations rather than merely existing, and they are engaging in ways that fulfill critical life goals while helping an organization achieve theirs. Thriving at work is rooted in positive psychology (Seligman, 2011; Seligman and Csikszentmihalyi, 2000), and it is different from a general sense of psychological well-being. Isaac Prilleltensky (2012), a well-known community psychologist, states that wellness, and its optimal state of thriving, is not only a function of biological and psychological determinants but is also created by social contexts where justice is permitted to exist.

You might remember from Chapter 1 that recent empirical work has shown that community experiences are correlated with employee thriving at work (Boyd and Nowell, 2020). A sense of community was found to be the strongest predictor of thriving at work compared with a sense of community responsibility, affective organizational commitment, organizational identification, and public service motivation. This recent study is important because it shows that creating organizational contexts where individuals psychologically experience a community (i.e., need fulfillment, membership, influence, and shared emotional connections) can lead to a human existence at work, and in life, that is characterized as life-affirming. It is interesting to note that Spreitzer et al. state (2005, p. 239), "when individuals are situated in particular work contexts they are more likely to thrive." They proposed that work unit contextual features include decision-making discretion, broad information sharing, a climate of trust and respect, and a climate of supervisor support.

These antecedents are similar to what we theorized would lead to community experiences almost 20 years ago, and recent empirical scholarship has borne that out. Social contextual features (i.e., like decision-making discretion and a climate of supervisor support) help to fulfill psychological needs of organizational members and, as we stated earlier, increase the fulfillment of the psychological contract. As needs are satiated, employees experience heightened psychological well-being, which simultaneously enables them to act with greater engagement toward their coworkers, the organization, and its stakeholders. Spreitzer et al. (2005) also note that a series of resources are produced as organizational members engage in work activity. When workers engage in task focus, exploration, and heedful relating, a variety of resources are produced (i.e., knowledge, positive meaning, positive affective resources, relational resources, and psychological capital), which generate greater levels of agentic activity (i.e., task focus, exploration, heedful relating) (Bandura, 2001). This so-called engine of thriving occurs by the circular interaction of agentic work activity with the resources it produces. It is interesting to conceptualize the interaction between community experiences and heedful relating (which are likely primarily cogenerated via positive affect and relational resources). Remember that when employees heedfully relate they are more able and likely to help others and provide social support (Spreitzer et al., 2005). And, by helping others and providing social support, psychological affect and physiological states are heightened. In other words, heedful relating is a concept that demands interconnection to others within a collective, it produces positive psychological and physical resources, and it appears to relate to helping behaviors toward others in the organization. In that sense, heedful relating is likely a concept that is directly created when leaders and managers build community at work. And, as the community experience model shows, once well-being, thriving, and engagement occur, outcomes like employee performance, development, absenteeism, tardiness, and turnover are impacted. Ultimately, these factors then likely influence organization-wide variables like efficiency, effectiveness, and responsiveness.

All organizations are collectives of individuals that in effect comprise a community. They are groups of people gathered for a common purpose who share some set of common beliefs and values. However, thriving communities at work are much more than collectives organized for a common purpose. They are settings where the human need for affiliation is satisfied through relationships with others in ways that are generated through trust, respect, mattering, inclusion, and dignity. Communities at work require social structures that promote and allow for membership, connection, and contribution; however, many of our social sources of community are in transition or disarray, or they no longer exist (Bellah et al., 1985; Heckscher, 2015). The Covid-19 pandemic and sharp increases in political divisiveness in recent years have added additional fractures toward goals of community at work. However, Block (2008), Hamel (2009), Mintzberg (2009), and Pfeffer (2018) have suggested that integrating community into organizations can assist in creating a sustainable future for organizations and society.

The idea of community in organizations has existed in the lexicon of organizational thinking for quite some time. For example, the Cadbury brothers famously built their "factory in a garden," where employees lived and worked in immediate proximity to create community well-being (Cadbury, 2010). Like Cadbury, Milton Hershey developed the town of Derry, Pennsylvania, where he grew up (now called Hershey, Pennsylvania), into a community of work where workers and executives lived directly across the street, and on adjacent company-owned parcels, to structurally design a flourishing community. The Cadbury and Hershey cases were especially interested in creating geographic structural communities that allowed individuals to live where they worked. Early 20th-century African American executive Charles C. Spaulding attempted to develop a company culture at North Carolina Mutual Life Insurance Company that embodied purpose, community, and aligned values (Prieto and Phipps, 2016, 2019).

Mary Parker Follett (1918) argued that the resolution to early 20th-century social problems—political and industrial—was in attending to humanity's inherent need for relatedness and belonging. Chester Barnard viewed "the condition of communion" (comradeship, social integration, mutual support) as essential to organizational effectiveness (Barnard, 1968, p. 148). Management scholars such as Drucker (1946), Argyris (1957), and Maslow (1965) referenced or advocated that a workplace should be a community, as have contemporary practitioners and scholars (Block, 2008; Chalofsky, 2010; Mintzberg, 2009; Pfeffer, 2018). However, none of this work has been specifically conceived within the logic of psychological experiences of community, and why proximate community experiences are central to our human existence at work.

Recent scholarship on community at work has changed the landscape of the management literature (e.g., Boyd and Nowell, 2017, 2020; Garrett, Spreitzer, and Bacevice, 2017; Livne-Tarandach and Jazaieri, 2021; Nowell and Boyd, 2014, 2010), and I believe that creating communities at work that specifically focus on psychological experiences of community will significantly help us truly build such settings. Leaders and managers, and those who are on a journey like Amanda, are at an inflection point in their thinking about a variety of social issues that permeate organizations today, and utilizing a science of community at work will help them toward realizing some of those lofty social justice goals. Amanda and others need concepts, frameworks, and theory about community at work. They also need evidence that shows that community experiences lead to important individual and collective outcomes. They also need measurements, tools, and techniques, and they need process and strategic approaches. Those things will come into focus as our journey together proceeds.

CHAPTER 3

It's Not All Roses and Defining and Measuring Community at Work

IT'S NOT ALL ROSES

A week later, Amanda is in her office checking emails when she gets a text from Ken. "Hey, honey, what time will you be home tonight?" Amanda replies, "I'm not sure yet. Probably 6ish." Ken writes back, "OK that should work. Remember we have to grab a quick dinner and then head over to your parents." "OK," Amanda says. What she doesn't say is that she totally forgot about going to her parents tonight, and she begins to contemplate whether she should keep the date or write back to Ken and tell him how swamped she is at work, and that they can reschedule for another day. But she doesn't do that and instead keeps working on emails. She's always been that way, and she expects that same from others around her. One of her father's famous sayings is "early to rise, early to succeed," and that has stuck with her in everything she does. Growing up, and even to this day, she tries to please her parents and wants their approval for achieving excellence in her life. That's why she was such a good youth soccer player, a National Honor Society student in high school, and someone who always tried to stay out of trouble. She never wanted to disappoint her parents. It is partly why she rises at 6:15 a.m. every day, even on weekends, and why she reads a chapter of a book every night before going to bed. "Each day should be productive. We're only here for a short time on earth, and we need to make the most of it" are common words that pass through her mind. At work, she tries to be a role model for others by coming in early and being one of the last people to leave each day. She has two basic rules for others around her: Be on time and be thorough in everything you do.

As she continues to scan through emails, she notices a memo from Sarah about their workers' compensation policy, and it reminds her of the

Building Community at Work. Neil Boyd, Oxford University Press. © Oxford University Press (2025).
DOI: 10.1093/9780197635964.003.0004

conversation last week in the boardroom about employee rumblings. She really is at a loss on this issue. She begins to contemplate a series of things. We pay above-market wages for almost all positions, especially at midmanagement and up. We have a 401K retirement plan with a 3% company match. We offer low-cost dental and vision care in addition to our preferred provider organization (PPO)/health maintenance organization (HMO) healthcare options. We give 2 weeks of vacation and 5 days of compensatory time (paid time off) for all employees. We promote from within (for the most part), and we donate to local community causes. As she goes through a laundry list of additional items, she eventually thinks to herself, "I just don't get it."

A few days later, she's in her office handling a contract dispute with a vendor when Sarah knocks on the door. "You have a minute?" Sarah says. Amanda replies, "Um, hold on one second . . . I need to finish this sentence of an email." After a brief pause, Amanda looks ups and says, "OK shoot, I'm good now." Sarah begins by telling Amanda that she has learned a bit more about the rumors that are going around. Sarah asked the operations director to put some feelers out, and he got back to her this morning. He says that some people, a decent amount, are feeling stressed. He says some employees are feeling the pressure of the production schedule, some are talking about a desire to take time off, but their supervisors are discouraging it because of the new apparel product rollouts, and he heard that lots of folks are upset because the company picnic was cancelled. "The company picnic?" Amanda exclaimed. "Don't they know how much that was costing us? And that we were able to keep doing some other things because we saved that money?" "I don't know," said Sarah. "I'm just the messenger." Amanda then asked, "So what do you think? Is there anything we can do?" Sarah began to tell Amanda about a recent talk at her local Society for Human Resource Management (SHRM) group that was about getting the most out of your employees. The bottom line of the event was that you need to talk with your employees. "Geez, that sounds awfully simple," Amanda said. "Well, it could be," Sarah replied, "but the advice of the speaker was to hire an external consultant who would come in and help us through the process." Amanda didn't like that answer. Consultants typically cost too much money, and she didn't think there were enough slack resources to afford one. Amanda asked, "Can we do this on our own?" Sarah replied, "Maybe . . . I think so. At least we can try, I guess." "OK, let's do it," Amanda said. Sarah then stated that she would investigate it a bit more and would report back in a few days. "We'll likely have to set up some discussions with different layers throughout the organization, and it will take some people away from their work, but it's probably worth it." "OK," Amanda replied, "But let's do our best to get this done efficiently and cheaply."

A couple of days later Amanda and Sarah met again, and Sarah began to describe a process for collecting information from employees. "Let's start at the top and work our way down," Sarah said. "The process will involve a one-hour conversation with the upper management team, and we will ask the mid-level managers to arrange similar-length conversations with the groups that report to them. Managers will take notes, and we'll compile all of the data in HR." Amanda liked the approach and thought it would bear some interesting fruit, but honestly, she believed that most of the data would say things were going well at the company. After a brief exchange about the process, and a side conversation related to new provisions in the healthcare plan, Sarah walked out of Amanda's office, and both of them went back to work.

Five days later, Amanda received an email from Sarah at 5:30 a.m. "We have to talk right away . . . it's about the data collection we're doing with employees." "OK, let's meet at 9:30 a.m., this morning. I have about 20 minutes then," said Amanda. At 9:30, Sarah knocked on her door, visibly breathing a little harder than normal. "What's up? You OK?" asked Amanda. Sarah took a deep breath,

> I'm fine, but I need to talk with you about what we're hearing from employees. It's not good. In almost every unit of the organization we are hearing that workers are dissatisfied, and the list is pretty big. I can share it with you later, but there are some major themes. People are saying this place has changed. That it used to be a much friendlier atmosphere, and that folks are feeling like cogs in a machine. They are complaining about their managers, their coworkers, and even us. There are lots of comments that you and the administrative team have taken the company in a direction that is not considerate of their needs. One good note, however, is that some employees are happy we asked their opinions and are hopeful things could change in the future.

Amanda was shocked. How could this be? What the heck was going on? How could anyone think such things about this company? Many questions like these were running through her mind as she directly stared at Sarah. "I know," Sarah said. "It's hard to believe." "It sure is," Amanda replied. The two of them discussed the issues in earnest over the next 10 minutes, and then Amanda said, "I'm really sorry, but I have to run to another meeting; let's carve out 45 minutes in our executive meeting on Friday to discuss this in detail. Can you create a presentation that we can use to kick-start the conversation?" "Sure, I can do that," said Sarah. And, with that, Amanda gathered her things and rushed out of the office.

At 10:00 a.m. that Friday, the executive meeting commenced. Sarah had her PowerPoint on the screen of the boardroom, clicker in hand, and was ready to go. Amanda started the meeting by thanking everyone for attending and reminded them that Sarah would be sharing some interesting information that was recently collected from employees. "Thank you for working on this,

Sarah," she said. "We're very much looking forward to hearing what you have learned." Sarah began by outlining the data collection process that was employed over the past couple of weeks. Next, she highlighted the key themes that emerged from the employee's conversations. "I hate to say this, but we have some unhappy campers!" Sarah exclaimed.

> The top three issues that recently emerged are that employees think we created a "worker-unfriendly culture," that managers are pushing them too hard and aren't sympathetic to their needs, and that we've lost touch with how the company used to be when it first started. For example, we have an employee who was upset that her manager would not intervene over a dispute she was having with another employee. Another employee is unhappy that we took away "dress-down" Fridays. And, almost everyone is upset that we cancelled the company picnic.

Amanda chimed in,

> What is up with the company picnic? When you mentioned that to me the other day, I didn't get it, and I still don't get it. We fully explained why we were cancelling the picnic, and we were clear that it was mostly because of excessive costs and too many liability concerns.

Several others offered similar comments and thoughts, but eventually Juan spoke up and said, "Perhaps it was just fun." Amanda immediately replied, "Fun? I get that, but fun isn't the first priority of a workplace. There are many more important things than just having fun. People don't understand what it's like to run a company, and they probably never will." Juan stayed silent while others professed similar sentiments to Amanda's about the state of current workers, especially younger ones who don't know what it's like to compete in the real world, and a series of dismissive comments that, in summary, amounted to a content thread that employees "just need to suck it up." After an hour of discussion, Amanda urged the group to move on to an update on recent sales and revenue data, but she offered that they should talk more about this issue at the executive meeting next week.

"So, did everyone have a good week since we last met?" Amanda said as she opened the executive session the following Friday. Most of the attendees replied with obligatory affirmative responses, although Jennifer, a sales director, mentioned that she turned 26 this week and it feels weird to be closing in on 30. "Ha! Wait 'til you hit 40!" Juan exclaimed as others chuckled around him. "You'll be there before you know it," said Amanda. "It's crazy how time flies when you're having fun, right everyone?" A few smirks and laughs were present in the room as Amanda took control of the meeting. "OK, so it's been a week since we talked about the employee findings that Sarah shared. What are we thinking? Jim, what do you think?" "Well, it's a tough one. I don't have any immediate silver bullets, but perhaps we should say something about it in public to the employees." Fred, the chief operating officer (COO), expressed that such a strategy could cause more problems than it's worth. "If you tell everyone that there is a collective sense of dissatisfaction, it could spread like a virus." Juan added, "Yeah, I can see that, but I can't imagine doing nothing about it. On the other hand, I'm not 100% sure what to do." "Sarah, you must have some ideas, what do you think?" Amanda added. "I agree with everything I've heard so far. We can't come right out and say there are big problems, and we can't ignore it. How about we prepare a statement that is somewhere in the middle and disseminate it to employees?" "That is a great idea," said Amanda. "Can you write a draft in the next couple of days, and then we'll work together to get it into shape?" "Sure, I'd be happy to do that," said Sarah.

On Wednesday of the following week, Amanda received an email from Sarah that contained the first draft of the employee statement. She opened the attached file and began reading:

> *Dear Employees,*
>
> *As you know, managers conducted a series of discussions with you over the past month. We are pleased to announce that we heard a lot of positive feedback from you, but we also learned that we can improve in certain areas. Rest assured that we heard you and we appreciate that you shared your opinions with us. The executive team will take your feedback into consideration and will work on solutions to ameliorate issues that are preventing us from reaching our full potential as an organization.*
>
> *Sincerely,*
>
> *Sarah Gleitner, Human Resources Director*

Amanda was very happy with the letter, and immediately wrote back to Sarah with a thumbs up. "Let's get this out today. I love it." Sarah did that, and at 4:00 p.m. the letter went out via email to everyone in the organization. Amanda was relieved. She was happy that they were taking action and that the executive team had reached a consensus of how to respond. She was sure this would quell any major problems or backlash and found herself thinking about the wonderful meatloaf dinner that was awaiting her this evening. It was her mother's recipe and one of her favorite meals. About 30 minutes later, she gathered up her computer and packed up her things. On her way out the office, she stopped at the break room to grab a water, and when she opened the door to enter, a conversation that was in midstream immediately stopped. "Don't let me interrupt you, keep on talking," she said wryly. "Ummm . . . that's OK, we were just about to leave for the day," said John, a marketing staffer who had been with the company for about a year. The other employees either looked away or began to get up and move toward the door. Amanda grabbed a water and headed back out the door she entered. As they exited on the other side of the room and the door was closing, she overheard one of them say under their breath, "Yeah . . . that letter from Sarah was a real doozy, wasn't it? Like we're going to believe that." Amanda could hear them all laugh as the door fell shut. It stopped her in her tracks. She immediately knew that she had a much bigger problem on her hands than she had anticipated.

Organizational life is not all roses for Amanda and her team, and the current cultural situation, and widespread dissatisfaction data from employees, is adding to the list of stressors that seem to be never-ending. You can see that Amanda is defensive about the findings, and because she isn't attuned to how critical this issue is, she would like to solve the problem quickly and efficiently and then just move on. But that's not how cultures of community work. They are built over time, through people, actions, policies, norms, and events, and they constantly need tending. As Schein (1992) described, organizational culture is enduring because it includes underlying beliefs and assumptions, shared values, and ways of interacting that contribute to the organization's social and psychological environment. Further, a strong sense of shared values, attitudes, and practices indicates the organization is a bounded unit and provides it with a distinct identity that influences the behavior of all members. Collecting employee perception data was a good step, but it certainly can't be the last action on a road toward co-creating a community with others in a collective setting. As I noted in Chapter 2, Amanda and her leadership team are likely not fully equipped to solve this problem, and they will need help to move forward on their journey toward realizing a thriving community.

On Monday of the following week, Amanda sends an email to an ex-professor of hers who taught the HR course during her MBA. She says,

> Good morning, Professor. I hope you are well. I was wondering if we could chat about a situation I'm having in my company? Might you be available to connect sometime this week? Tuesday or Wednesday afternoon is especially good for me, so let me know if you might be able to do it. My best, Amanda.

Later that day, Professor Jenkins writes back,

> Hello Amanda! It is wonderful to hear from you. I heard about the great successes of your company, and I'd be more than happy to chat with you. I'll send you a Google Invite for Wednesday at 2:30 p.m., and we can chat over Zoom. Talk soon, John. P.S. Feel free to call me John in the future. :).

The chat with John leads to a variety of insights for Amanda. He mentions advanced courses he teaches in organizational behavior, including one on organizational culture that he's taught for the past 10 years, and a new one he recently developed titled Inclusive Leadership. He tells Amanda that she could have enrolled in the organizational culture course as an elective during her MBA, but students who focus on accounting and finance don't usually take it. He listens intently to Amanda as she describes the situation at work, and after a series of back-and-forth dialogues he says,

> I think you need help. I have a friend and colleague, Susan, who you should meet. She worked for Deloitte Consulting in their Human Capital practice for the last 7 years, and she recently started a small consulting firm in the area where she's been helping clients with various issues that relate to human and people issues in organizations.

Amanda reacted by stating, "Are you sure, John? Do I really need to hire a consultant? I feel like I could be wasting money." John replied, "Yes, I strongly urge you to meet with her and hear what she has to say. And, don't consider it wasting money. Look at it as an investment. An investment into the most important aspect of your company: Its people!"

Amanda agrees to talk with Susan, and a week later, they meet in Amanda's office. Susan is introduced by Amanda's assistant, Sarina, and they each take a comfortable seat around a round coffee table. "Would you like something to drink, Susan? Coffee, tea, water, something else?" "Some water would be nice," Susan replied. "Wonderful, coming right up," Amanda responded. As the discussion began, Amanda explained the situation. She told Susan about the company, its incredible growth over the past several years, the pressures of trying to run the organization, and the recent attempt of listening to employee complaints. Susan took it all in, asked lots of probing questions, and after 30 minutes of discussion said,

> I think I can help you, but you would have to be willing to go through a process. The first thing I'd like to do is teach you about measuring community at work. Last year, I attended the Academy of Management Conference, which is the largest annual gathering of management scholars, where I learned about the community experience model, and various measurement techniques that can be used to gather employee data. I've been using the model in my consulting practice, and I think we should use it. There is a lot more we should discuss, but if you're up for it, let's get started. I'll send you a proposal, and you can get back to me.

And, with that, they ended the meeting and wished each other a pleasant rest of the day.

A couple of days later, Amanda received the proposal from Susan via email. Cost was at the top of her mind as she opened the PDF, and she immediately looked at the budget on Page 5. "Oh, wow, this isn't cheap, but it's not as bad as I thought it would be." After a careful read of the full proposal, Amanda thought, "I really like that Susan is willing to integrate her work with things our HR Department can do, which will help us keep the cost down. And, overall, I'm impressed with what Susan has to offer." She wrote back to Susan and expressed that she'd like to get started, but she also asked if they could set up the work contract in stages so they could assess how things were going between the parties along the way. Susan agreed to that arrangement, and she then began the process by helping Amanda, and her team, understand how they might improve the measurement of community by grounding data collection in the community experience model.

DEFINING AND MEASURING COMMUNITY AT WORK

Measuring employee perceptions that are anchored to the community experience model requires various nodes of thinking. First, as you will learn in Chapter 4, Susan will highlight that a consulting process model will be needed, and it will likely be co-created with Amanda and her leadership team by grounding it in organizational development and change models like participatory action research (which is also commonly used by community psychologists for social and organizational change work), appreciative inquiry, and design thinking, or a modification of Deloitte's consulting process model, which includes Agile sprints (e.g., multiple iterations of prototypes over a series of weeks). Second, no matter which process model they employ, they will need to collect preliminary data in the early stages of the project to assess whether the "presenting problem" (if using an action research approach) or "the vision of a better future" (if using appreciative inquiry) is correctly aligned to community at work. After reviewing the data that Sarah and her HR team collected, Susan is convinced that a focus on community experiences is appropriate. In order to prepare Amanda and her team for a deeper investigation into community experiences, Susan begins with a couple of executive sessions where she teaches the group about the community experience model, and how they might go about understanding how to measure a sense of community and a sense of community responsibility.

Measurement of psychological constructs from a social sciences perspective is an interesting endeavor because various scholars would employ different data collection methodologies depending on their orientation toward research. On the one hand, qualitative researchers would tend to favor interviews, focus groups, observation, archival data collection, and other methods that allow them to learn from comments and textual data. Qualitative data tend to be rich and nuanced. On the other hand, quantitative researchers would favor surveys, quantitative output and outcome data, data inside EXCEL sheets, and other ways of understanding that emanate from numbers. Quantitative data tend to be less rich and nuanced, but it tends to be more efficient to collect, and quantitative scales have an appearance of validity because they can be statistically analyzed. Scholars have their preferences for data collection that have been shaped by their graduate school mentors, and by the norms of scholarly practices of the times (e.g., quantitative methods have been favored in recent times compared with qualitative analysis in psychology and management), but an open and inclusive scholarship community believes that both qualitative and quantitative scholarship have value. Some scholars use qualitative assessment as their primary method of data collection due to their training and worldviews, and others use it in the early stages of a research agenda when conducting exploratory studies to help shape the direction of later quantitative research.

Management consultants and community psychologists who employ social science research techniques tend to use a toolbelt of methods. For example, it is common to begin preliminary data collection with interviews and observation, and as a project progresses, to add focus groups, surveys, and other techniques that could be either qualitative or quantitative based on the joint planning of the consultant and the client. In short, while management consultants do have individual preferences for data collection techniques, practitioners are more often agnostic to data collection methods compared with academic scholars.

In the case of grounding measurement schemes to the community experience model, I would suggest (as Susan does), that the project could begin with qualitative or quantitative measures, or a mix of both strategies. A qualitative approach would normally begin by developing open-ended questions that would directly link to the community experience model. Remember from Chapter 1 that the model has a series of components. At its core, psychological community experiences are defined as a sense of community (that includes elements of membership, influence, need fulfillment, and shared emotional connection), and a sense of community responsibility. Each of these experiences can lead to psychological and behavioral outcomes for individuals, work units, the organization, and stakeholders outside the organization. Finally, a sense of community is primarily created as resources in the organizational context are provided that satisfy membership, influence, basic and other needs, and shared emotional connections, and a sense of community responsibility is created as one enters an organization with a predisposition for responsibility toward others, and as one's normative stance interacts with the organizational context in a way that either facilitates or thwarts cognitions of wanting to care and act on behalf of the collective. A measurement system that is grounded in the community experience model would therefore ask questions about *Antecedent Resources and Beliefs in the Organizational Context*, *Sense of Community/Sense of Community Responsibility*, and *Outcomes*.

For example, one might ask things like "Do you think community at work matters? What does community at work mean to you? Can you explain how you feel about your membership, influence, need fulfillment, and shared emotional connections at work?" Of course, these items could be further developed and refined as needed, but notice how elements of the questions directly link to the constructs of a sense of community (i.e., membership, need fulfillment, influence, shared emotional connections), and to a sense of community responsibility. Notice how a question like "What factors around you at work are getting in the way of you feeling a sense of community, or, can you express what it would take for you to experience a sense of community responsibility for your coworkers, the organization, and its stakeholders?" is targeted at the organizational context that can lead to community experiences. Or, notice how a question like "When you feel like a member of your work unit, what gets better?" aligns with individual and higher order outcomes that a sense of community should predict. The point here is that measurement grounding in the community experience model will significantly improve the questions you develop, and as scholars know well, good questions often lead to good data. In Chapter 4, I will expand the discussion of qualitative research and link it to organizational development and change modeling, show you recent research findings that were based on qualitative research, and use that data as fodder for what Susan and others are learning in Amanda's company. I will also provide more information about how to conduct qualitative assessments, but for now, we turn our attention to a variety of quantitative measurement systems that have been built by scholars in the fields of community psychology and management over the past 35 years. When it comes to measuring community experiences, the academic literature has a long history in the development of psychological scales, and over the past several decades, the implementation of such scales has been the primary mode by which community experiences have been measured. Susan reviewed this history during her kick-off meeting with the leadership team, and I think you should learn about these measurement systems too.

A History of Measuring a Sense of Community

Remember from Chapter 1 that a sense of community was the only community experience construct in the academic literature until Nowell and Boyd (2014, 2010) discovered that a sense of community responsibility also contributes to the totality of community experiences in collective settings. Therefore, since the initial conceptualization of a sense of community by Sarason (1974) and construct refinement by McMillan and Chavis (1986), measurement development was exclusively focused on a sense of community. Many measures for a sense of community have been developed over the years, and the vast majority of them anchor to the McMillan and Chavis (1986) framework (i.e., membership, influence, need fulfillment, shared emotional connection). Historically, all of the measures typically used a residential community referent (e.g., town, neighborhood, or block) or have been created or translated for use in specific countries (e.g., Italy). Most of them have not gained a specific dominance in the academic literature or have been adapted for organizational settings. Thus, I describe several sense-of-community measures that have been extensively employed in academic science, or in practice, and have been commonly used in my work, or in the work of others who have explored community constructs in organizations. I also introduce a more recent scale that holds promise for application in organizational settings. These measures include the Sense of Community Index (SCI; and its update the SCI-2), the Brief Sense of Community Index (BSCI), the Brief Sense of Community scale (BSCS), and the Psychological Sense of Community scale (PSCS).

The Sense of Community Index (SCI) and the SCI-2

As Long and Perkins (2003) note, the SCI was developed in the mid-1980s by community psychologist David Chavis with the assistance of several other researchers (Paul Florin, Doug Perkins, John Prestby, Richard Rich, and Abraham Wandersman) who were working on the New York City Block Booster action research project. In the early years of sense-of-community measurement, and perhaps true in total since 1986, the SCI has been the most used scale in academic science to measure a sense of community. David Chavis, who founded Community Science (https://communityscience.com/) and is the CEO and principal associate, explains that the SCI is the most frequently used quantitative measure of sense of community in the social sciences. The scale has been used all over the world and in many collective contexts (e.g., urban, suburban, rural, tribal, workplaces, schools, universities, recreational clubs, Internet communities, etc., and the scale has been employed prodigiously in practice settings (see Table 3.1). You will notice that the scale uses referents of a "block" or "neighborhood," but modifying the referent to an organization, a division, a work unit, or group can easily be done.

After the publication and use of the SCI, a series of research studies questioned whether or not the SCI could appropriately measure its intended four dimensions. For example, Chipuer and Pretty (1999) reported modest reliability scores for the SCI and even less consistent reliability for the four subscales. In addition, they measured the SCI across various samples (with adolescents and adults; in neighborhoods and in a workplace), and their results did not provide consistent four-dimension factor structures across the samples, nor did they fully align to the McMillan and Chavis (1986) framework. Another study by Long and Perkins (2003), which revisited and analyzed the original data set from the New York City Block Booster project, failed to confirm the four-dimensional factor structure and called into question the reliability and efficacy of the SCI.

In 2008, Chavis, Lee, and Acosta revisited the SCI scale, and even though they believed the original 12-item SCI scale had been adequate, they acknowledged that the reliability of the four subscales could be empirically low and inconsistent. They further acknowledged that critics of the SCI were especially concerned about the true–false response set that limited statistical variability, and its adequacy as a cross-cultural measure. In their study, they tested the reliability and validity of a new 24-item SCI-2 that used a 4-point Likert-type scale instead of a true–false response format. Contrary to the SCI, the SCI-2 was able to align with the four factors in the McMillan and Chavis (1986) framework, and the authors showed that the scale had excellent reliability. While the SCI-2 has been extensively used by Community Science, and by other practitioners (go to http://www.senseofcommunity.com/ to seek permission and sign an agreement form to gain access to the scale), it has not been consistently employed as a measure in academic research studies since its inception. One reason for this fact is that factor-analytic studies produced alternatives to the SCI and the SCI-2, and they have gained greater application in the academic literature.

Table 3.1 THE SENSE OF COMMUNITY INDEX

True or false
I think my block is a good place for me to live.
People on this block do not share the same values.
My neighbors and I want the same things from the block.
I can recognize most of the people who live on my block.
I feel at home on this block.
Very few of my neighbors know me.
I care about what my neighbors think of my actions.
I have almost no influence over what this block is like.
If there is a problem on this block people who live here can get it solved.
It is very important to me to live on this particular block.
People on this block generally don't get along with each other.
I expect to live on this block for a long time.

Source: Chavis, D.M., Hogge, J.H., McMillan, D.W., & Wandersman, A. (1986). Sense of community through Brunswick's lens: A first look. *Journal of Community Psychology*, 14(1), 24–40.

Brief Sense of Community Index and Brief Sense of Community Scale

The SCI and the SCI-2 were intended to be brief instruments that assessed the four dimensions of the McMillan and Chavis (1986) model. As noted earlier, community psychology scholars especially challenged the factor structure and reliability of the SCI because of its persistence of use within academic studies. Some also challenged whether the SCI was actually brief enough. A 24-item scale doesn't seem especially long, unless you are also attempting to measure a variety of other constructs in the midst of a research study. When several measures need to be collected, it would be preferable to have fewer items (as long as they can be validated and are reliable). Long and Perkins (2003) applied more advanced statistical methods to the original data set in which the SCI was first developed (i.e., confirmatory factor analysis [CFA]), and beyond confirming problems with the instrument, they added additional items that were not part of the original SCI, and their inclusion provided a better factor structure and reliability. They recommended that researchers not use the SCI and instead argued that scholars should use the eight-item BSCI (see Table 3.2).

The eight items aligned to a new conceptual structure with three dimensions: *social connections*, *mutual concerns*, and *community values*. However, scholars like Obst and White (2004) and Petersen, Speer, and McMillan (2008) proposed that Long and Perkins (2003) did not adequately provide theoretical justification for the new three-factor structure. In addition, Petersen et al. (2008) noted that an important step forward would include testing new original items based on the McMillan and Chavis (1986) framework. Their study produced an eight-item BSCS, which measured need fulfillment, membership, influence, and emotional connection (see Table 3.3). Like most things in life, there is a lot more to the measurement story of a sense of community, but suffice it to say that the Petersen et al. (2008) BSCS gained considerable traction in the academic literature, and it has been employed in many different community settings.

The Psychological Sense of Community Scale (PSCS)

I also want to introduce you to a new measure of sense of community that Jason, Stevens, and Ram (2015) proposed to the academic literature: the PSCS, which is based on three distinct ecological domains involving the individual, microsystem, and macrosystem (see Table 3.4). Factor analytic techniques were used to derive a scale that measures three theoretical domains involving Self (identity and importance to self), Membership (social relationships),

Table 3.2 THE BRIEF SENSE OF COMMUNITY INDEX

	BSCI	SCI
I can recognize most of the people who live on my block.	Social connections	Membership
Very few of my neighbors know me.	Social connections	Membership
I have almost no influence over what this block is like.	Social connections	Influence
My neighbors and I want the same things from the block.	Mutual concerns	Need fulfillment
If there is a problem on this block people, who live here can get it solved.	Mutual concerns	Influence
In general, would you say that people on your block watch after each other and help out when they can, or do they pretty much go their own way?	Mutual concerns	
Would you say that it is very important, somewhat important, or not important to you to feel a sense of community with the people on your block?	Community values	
Would you say that you feel a strong sense of community with others on your block, very little sense of community, or something in between?	Community values	

Note. BSCI, Brief Sense of Community Index; SCI: Sense of Community Index. Original items, Perkins et al. (1990); measures, McMillan and Chavis's (1986) four-component theoretical structure. If an SCI cell is blank in the table, it means that this was new item added by Long and Perkins (2003). For the SCI, respondents were instructed to indicate whether the statement is mostly true or mostly false about their street block. For the new items, the response options were contained in the questions.

and Entity (a group's organization and purpose). Like others before them, the authors expressed that we need measurement instruments that both theoretically represent an individual's experience of community and are empirically reliable and valid. They note that their scale has utility compared with a variety of others because it is grounded in an ecological framework that allows for quantifying multidimensional units of analysis instead of only measuring perceptions at the individual level. However, given the newness of the scale, we do not yet know how or if it will hold up across studies and settings, but it might be a promising advance in sense-of-community measurement.

Recommendations for Measuring a Sense of Community

When Branda and I began to empirically study community experiences in organizational settings we used the BSCS quite a bit, and we altered the referent to "organization" or "work unit." We used it because we were collecting data on a variety of other measures in addition to sense of community, and a brief scale made sense in that context. Interestingly, we were not able to validate the four-factor structure of the scale like Petersen et al. (2008), but we were able to validate the instrument as a unidimensional measure of sense of community. In one of our studies, we attempted to use the SCI (with the referent adjusted

Table 3.3 BRIEF SENSE OF COMMUNITY SCALE

	McMillan and Chavis Dimension
I can get what I need in this neighborhood	Need fulfillment
This neighborhood helps me fulfill my needs	Need fulfillment
I feel like a member of this neighborhood	Membership
I belong in this neighborhood	Membership
I have a say about what goes on in my neighborhood	Influence
People in this neighborhood are good at influencing each other	Influence
I feel connected to this neighborhood	Emotional Connection
I have a good bond with others in this neighborhood	Emotional Connection

Note. All Brief Sense of Community Scale (BSCS) items were designed to reference respondents' neighborhood and used a 5-point, Likert-type response option format ranging from strongly agree to strongly disagree.

to an "organization"), and we had a very hard time validating individual items and the four-factor structure of the scale.

Therefore, at this point, I recommend that several scales could be useful for quantitatively assessing sense of community. First, the BSCS has been used the most in academic studies, and it has been validated more often in the academic literature than any scale that has been employed in quantitative studies. Even though it has not always held up in ways that allow for confidence in its four-factor structure, I believe that it is a good brief measure for a sense of community that is grounded in the McMillan and Chavis (1986) framework. Second, the SCI-2 has been used extensively in community practice (especially by Community Science), and it has appeared to work well for many community practitioners and scientists. One would have to consider whether a 24-item scale is too large for a specific application, but given the ongoing debates about measurement reliability and validity of sense-of-community scales in the academic literature, we believe the SCI-2 is a worthy option for administration. Finally, I believe that the PSCS is a potential option if you are interested in measuring multiple referents at a time from an ecological analysis framework. We need more academic studies to confirm that the PSCS is a reliable and valid measure, but again, given the intellectual questions about all of the sense-of-community measures, we believe that the PSCS could be effectively employed as a measure in organizational settings.

Measuring a Sense of Community Responsibility

In addition to a sense of community, the community experience model posits that a sense of community responsibility is an important construct that

Table 3.4 THE PSYCHOLOGICAL SENSE OF COMMUNITY SCALE (PSCS)

Using this measure, first replace the letter "E" with the Entity and the letter "M" with the Membership that the sample will refer to. Respondents answer whether they *Strongly Disagree, Disagree, Slightly Disagree, Slightly Agree, Agree,* or *Strongly Agree* with the questions below.

Entity

I think this E was a good E.
I did not leave this E because I wanted to.
For me, this E was a good fit.

Membership

M could depend on each other in this E.
M could get help from other.
M if they needed it
M were secure in sharing opinions or asking for advice.

Self

This E was important to me.
I made friends in this E.
I felt good helping the E and the M.

The questions above are in the past tense, so if an investigator decides to use this scale for a person's current sense of community, we suggest using the slight variation of wording below that puts things in the present tense.

Entity

I think this E is a good E.
I am not planning on leaving this E.
For me, this E is a good fit.

Membership

M can depend on each other in this E.
M can get help from other.
M if they need it
M are secure in sharing opinions or asking for advice.

Self

This E is important to me.
I have friends in this E.
I feel good helping the E and the M.

captures experiences of community in collective settings. Branda and I (Nowell and Boyd, 2014, 2010) were the first to propose and empirically validate that a sense of community responsibility is a unique construct of a sense of community (as opposed to a fifth dimension of McMillan and Chavis's framework). A sense of community responsibility is grounded in normative values and beliefs of responsibility toward others in a collective, the collective itself, and external stakeholders to the collective. Our early qualitative work led to the development of the Sense of Community Responsibility Scale (SCRS), which was first used in a study of a statewide healthcare network in North Carolina (Nowell and Boyd, 2014). Over the course of several empirical studies, we have used variations of the original scale that either subtlety modified the nuanced wording of a particular item or altered the referent. Notice in Table 3.5 how the scale has been modified to focus on an organization, a department, a work unit, or an external stakeholder (one would need to specify customer, citizen, client, or some other specific stakeholder). Like us, you (or Amanda) would need to modify the specific referent for your needs. You should also know that we have measured multiple referents within the same study a couple of times (e.g., the work unit and the organization), and you might want to do that if you are interested in understanding community experiences at multiple levels of analysis within or across organizations.

Finally, I would like to share an additional variation of the Sense of Community Responsibility Scale (SCRS), which was produced by Treitler et al. (2018). They conducted a study that applied item response theory to examine the psychometric properties of the SCRS (Nowell and Boyd, 2014) in an evaluation of community-based substance abuse prevention coalitions. Findings of the study showed that the SCRS was reliable, was unidimensional, and functioned well, particularly at low and moderate levels of the construct. They also showed that the addition of two items intended to capture higher levels of a sense of community responsibility improved the scale's functioning at the higher levels. Their work provided empirical evidence to support the reliability and validity of the SCRS scale. Like all of the sense-of-responsibility scales, their variation would require alteration of the referent because as you can see in Table 3.5, they only applied the referent of a "regional coalition."

Concluding Thoughts About Measuring Community Experiences

As you can see by the discussion in this chapter, Amanda, you, and others, have a variety of options in measuring community experiences. Both qualitative and quantitative approaches can be employed, and a rich history of academic science and practice has contributed to our understanding of how to measure community at work. Qualitative approaches are especially useful toward understanding rich and deep meaning of community experiences, and we believe they can be used in an exploratory mode or to confirm the existence of particular aspects of community at work. Quantitative techniques are especially useful to capture lots of data in shorter periods of time, and they lend themselves to easy modification and application in a variety of settings. They also help us quickly see how a collective and individuals in a collective are experiencing community at work (e.g., via measures of central tendency and variability), and they are excellent measures when attempting to correlate, predict, or serve as

Table 3.5 SENSE OF COMMUNITY RESPONSIBILITY SCALE

Original items (Nowell and Boyd, 2014)

Relative to other collaboratives I have belonged to, I feel more strongly about supporting the members in this collaborative.

One of the best things my organization can do to improve community health is to be of service to this collaborative.

Relative to other collaboratives I've been involved with, I feel a particularly strong sense of responsibility for the success of this collaborative.

I am always ready to help out people in this collaborative even if it creates hardship for me.

I feel a strong personal obligation to improve this collaborative.

I feel it is my duty to give to this collaborative without needing to receive anything in return.

Recently used variation in multiple studies

It is easy for me to put aside my own agenda in favor of the greater good of my [*organization, department, work unit, external stakeholder*].

When volunteers are needed by my [*organization, department, work unit, external stakeholder*], I feel like I should be one of the first to step up.

I feel it is my duty to give to my [*organization, department, work unit, external stakeholder*] without needing to receive anything in return.

I am always ready to help out people in my [*organization, department, work unit, external stakeholder*], even if it creates hardship for me.

I often feel an obligation to do things that benefit my [*organization, department, work unit, external stakeholder*], even if my costs outweigh any personal benefit I may receive.

One of the best things I can do to improve my [*organization, department, work unit, external stakeholder*] is to be of service to my [*organization, department, work unit, external stakeholder*].

Treitler, Peterson, Howell, and Powell (2018) eight-item version

Relative to other community groups I have belonged to, I feel more strongly about supporting the members in this *Regional Coalition.*

One of the best things I can do to improve community health is to be of service to this *Regional Coalition.*

Relative to other community organizations I've been in involved with, I feel a particularly strong sense of responsibility for the success of this *Regional Coalition.*

I am always ready to help out people in this *Regional Coalition* even if it creates hardship for me.

I feel a strong personal obligation to improve this *Regional Coalition.*

I feel it is my duty to give to this *Regional Coalition* without needing to receive anything in return.

I would be willing to pay a high personal cost for the good of this *Regional Coalition.*

I am always among the first to sacrifice my interests if it is important to the *Regional Coalition's* mission.

Note. Respondents typically indicate their agreement to each of the items based on a 7-point Likert-type scale ranging from strongly disagree to strongly agree; however, 5-point Likert-type scales have also been used.

outcome variables. For example, quantitative scales can help us determine if particular antecedents statistically predict community experiences, and they can help us understand the kinds of outcomes that community experiences can statistically predict.

General complementary social science or management research methods and statistical knowledge and skills are helpful too because they can increase the likelihood of effective design, implementation, and analysis of any kind of data one might collect. I would strongly urge any user of the quantitative or qualitative measurement techniques to consult with individuals holding such expertise when attempting to measure community experiences in academic or applied projects. This is what Susan will provide as she helps Amanda and her organization come to grips with the rumblings at work, how those complaints can be conceived using the community experience model, and how various measurement techniques can be employed to isolate variables that can lead to the design of a thriving community at work.

CHAPTER 4

Seeking Help and Planning to Build Community

SEEKING HELP

A few days after the kickoff session with Susan, Amanda is having dinner at home with Ken and the kids. "Thank goodness it's Friday," says Ken. "Yeah, I agree, it's been a long week. I'm looking forward to relaxing a little bit this weekend," Amanda replied. "And, I can't wait to go skating tomorrow," exclaimed Gabby. Amanda paused for a second as she contemplated getting up at 7:00 a.m. to take Gabby to a skating lesson and then replied, "Me too honey, it's going to be so much fun." Later in the day on Saturday the family is planning to go to the park, and Ken is eager to show Jensen some of the new playground equipment that was installed in the nature-learning area at the park. On Sunday, they plan to go to church and visit with some friends in the afternoon, who also have small kids. As Amanda contemplates the activities of the weekend, she is filled with content, but she also knows that her time to relax will be limited. She is happy to spend some quality time with Ken and the kids and wants to be present in everything they do this weekend. She also has a lot on her mind about work. "So how is the consultant working out?" Ken asks. "Funny you should ask. I was just thinking about that," she replied. "It's interesting. I didn't think I needed her, but I've had a change of heart. I think she is going to add value." "BORING," exclaimed Gabby. "Haha, you're right sweetie. Let's not talk about work. Let's talk about tomorrow," said Amanda. The conversation shifted to a discussion of what Gabby would wear for skating, the fact that she was excited to wear her new pearl white skates, and that the gumball machine might spit out a blue sugary treat at the indoor rink. They also talked about Kara, Gabby's skating instructor. "I'm gonna see Kara and show her that I can do that spin," Gabby announced. "That's right," said Ken. "You're gonna do it!" "And, when I do it, you're going to clap. Just like on TV," she replied. "You bet we will," said Amanda. "And we'll make sure Jensen claps too!" "Mommy,

Building Community at Work. Neil Boyd, Oxford University Press. © Oxford University Press (2025).
DOI: 10.1093/9780197635964.003.0005

can we bring Pooh Bear, too? I want him to see me skate." "Sure, we can do that," said a smiling Amanda. "And, maybe Kara can show him a few tricks." As Amanda basked in the glow of a conversation through a child's eye, she thought about the necessity of having Kara teach Gabby how to skate. Neither Ken nor she had any formal training in skating even though they were more than able to stay upright when engaging in the sport. She thought to herself, "Yeah, I guess seeking help makes sense when you're not sure what to do."

After a fun and active weekend, Amanda is back in the office on Monday, and she has a 9:00 a.m. meeting with Susan. They are chatting about next steps, and Susan asks, "So what do you think about the process so far?" "I think the first session went well," Amanda replied.

> I like that we have a roadmap in terms of how to conceptualize community, and I thought the various measurement options made a lot of sense. To be honest, though, I'm a little bit unsure on how the entire process might unfold. Perhaps you could talk a little bit about that?

"Sure, I'm happy to do that," replied Susan. "I'll give you a primer now, and then I think we should present this information, in more detail, at a meeting with others next week." "Sounds good," Amanda replied.

A Management Consulting Process

Management consulting has evolved from many different angles and disciplines over time, but many point to the work of Kurt Lewin in the 1930s–1940s with participatory action research, and how it shaped the early era of the field of organization development and change (Cummings and Worley, 2015). Interestingly, community psychologists also point to Lewin as an intellectual thought leader in social change theory and social change research methodology (Boyd, 2014; Boyd and Angelique, 2002; Hart and Bond, 1995; Lewin, 1946), which many community psychology scholars use when conducting research studies or engaging in community consulting (e.g., see Kelly et al., 2004; Lykes, 2017). In the late 1930s, Kurt Lewin, a social psychologist, conducted quasi-experimental tests in factory and neighborhood settings to demonstrate that democratic participation enhanced productivity, and law and order, compared with autocratic coercion (Adelman, 1993). Lewin showed that action research could stimulate social relationships of groups, and between groups, to sustain communication and cooperation. Action research was the means of a systematic inquiry for all participants with a goal of greater effectiveness through democratic participation. He promoted the use of social science as a method to help solve social conflicts and showed how action research could produce reflective thought, discussion, decision, and action by ordinary people participating in collective research (Wright Mills, 1959).

This early work led to Lewin's famous development of psychological sensitivity training and T-groups (Lewin, 1951; a form of training that helps people become more aware of their own goals as well as their prejudices, and more sensitive to others and to the dynamics of group interaction), which is often characterized as the beginning of management consulting and organization development and change as we know it today (Cummings and Worley, 2015). Of course, there were others before Lewin who influenced the development of management consulting, including Frederick Taylor's scientific management; the famous Hawthorne studies at Western Electric in Cicero, Illinois; Mary Parker Follet's work on democratizing collective settings; and Chester Barnard's focus on cooperative organizations (Wren and Bedeian, 2020). Each of these scholars ultimately influenced management science and practice, which set the stage for a modern management consulting field. However, Lewin is clearly regarded as having an enormous influence on early management consulting in promoting research that could lead to action in organizations.

In 1946, Kurt Lewin, a faculty member at MIT and director of the Research Center for Group Dynamics, was asked by the director of the Connecticut State Interracial Commission to conduct a training with the goal of improving leadership and interracial issues. Lewin gathered a group of trainers and researchers, and that summer, they conducted a workshop that included lectures, role play, and group discussions. In the evenings, some of the leaders and attendees discussed participant behavior during the sessions of the day. This unplanned activity led to a variety of helpful insights. For example, some participants disagreed with insights of the trainers and researchers, and Lewin recognized that participant observations were not part of any planned data collection methodology. The next day, the group decided to continue with these discussions, and it quickly became apparent that the discussions of participant behavior were more insightful than any of the planned activities of the training. From this humble origin sprang what was eventually labeled sensitivity training, T-groups, and laboratory training, and it sparked the field of organization development and change.

In the subsequent decades to Lewin's initial insight of the value of directly reporting feedback to participants, his work influenced the development of management consulting process models and measurement techniques. After his untimely death on February 12, 1947, at the age of 57, later in the year, the Research Center for Group Dynamics moved to the University of Michigan. In 1946, Rensis Likert created the Center for Survey Research at Michigan, and when the Center for Group Dynamics moved there, he led both efforts. Rensis Likert is well known for the development of the 5-point Likert scale that we all have experienced when taking surveys. He was the first to develop scales that measured human perceptions and attitudes during his doctoral dissertation at Michigan, and after joining the faculty, his efforts led to wide-scale applications of survey feedback for improving group dynamics in organizations. The combination of early sensitivity training and feedback to participants through observation or survey methods were both part of the early origins of what we now call management consulting process models.

Kurt Lewin is often characterized as developing the first consulting process model that included the stages of *unfreezing*, *movement*, and *refreezing* (Lewin, 1947; see Table 4.1). Like the participants who attended sensitivity training, individuals and the organizations they inhabit can get stuck and "frozen" in a status quo of habitual thinking and behavior. Status quo thinking and action are often associated with an inability to see a new and better way of doing things, and behavioral habits, as we all know, are difficult to change. Most of what we call "resistance to change" is especially rooted in us holding onto our cognitive and behavioral habits because of convenience, and perhaps a skepticism that changing our behavior is actually in our best interest and the interest of the organization. Lewin was keenly aware of the problem of the status quo, and he prodigiously wrote about the necessity of "unfreezing" status quo perceptions, attitudes, thinking, and behavior. Feedback from observers and data were useful tools for insight, and as stimulation for the possibility that "moving" to a new state through cognitive and behavioral action was warranted. Once the individual had moved to the new state, it was important for the "change agent" to help the individual, group, or organization "refreeze" that new state into an institutionalized way of behaving that would be repeatable and solidified.

Table 4.1 MANAGEMENT CONSULTING PROCESS MODELS

Lewin's model	Action research	Appreciative inquiry
Unfreezing	Problem identification	Discover
		Appreciate "what is"
	Consult with behavioral science expert(s)	
	Data gathering and preliminary diagnosis	Dream
		Imagine "what might be"
Movement	Feedback to key client group	
	Joint diagnosis of the problem	Design
		Determine "What could be"
Refreeze	Joint action planning	
	Action/intervention	Deliver
		Create "What will be"
	Data after action/evaluation	

Over time, Lewin's original change model was modified into what is commonly termed *traditional action research*, which tends to be associated with the following basic steps (adapted from Cummings and Worley, 2015; see also French and Bell, 1994; Schein, 1988):

Problem identification: This stage usually begins when a key executive in the organization, or someone with power and influence, senses that the organization or system has one or more problems that might be solved with the help of a professional facilitator or an organizational development and change (ODC) practitioner. Contemporary approaches to problem identification expressly include input about potential problems by any stakeholder within, or around, the organization.

Consultation with a behavioral science expert: During the initial contact, the ODC practitioner and the client carefully assess each other. During this sharing stage, the client and consultant seek to establish an open and collaborative atmosphere.

Data gathering and preliminary diagnosis: This step involves gathering appropriate information and analyzing it to determine the underlying causes of organizational problems. Typically, interviews, process observation, questionnaires, and organizational performance data are collected.

Feedback to a key client or group: The feedback step, in which organizational members are given information by the ODC practitioner, helps them determine the strengths and weaknesses of the organization or department under study.

Joint diagnosis of the problem: At this point, members discuss the feedback and explore with the ODC practitioner whether they want to work on identified problems. A close relationship exists during data gathering, feedback, and diagnosis because the consultant summarizes the basic data from the client members and presents the data to them for validation and further diagnosis.

Joint action planning: Next, the ODC practitioner and client members jointly agree on further actions to be taken. This is the moving process that Lewin described.

Action: This stage involves the actual change effort. It may include installing new methods and procedures, reorganizing structures and work designs, and reinforcing new behaviors.

Data gathering after action: Because action research is a cyclical process, data must also be gathered after the action has been taken to measure and determine the effects of the action and to feed the results back to the organization.

These steps, in turn, may lead to rediagnosis and new action. You can see in these steps a clear bias toward a priority on identifying and resolving problems. Note, for instance, the two uses of the terms, *diagnosis* and *problem identification*, which imply that something is wrong within the system. The underlying metaphor of these activities is that an individual, group, or organization is sick or in a state of ailment, requiring a need for healing and restoration to be made whole (Boyd and Bright, 2007). The consultant in an action research process often takes on the role of a physician who can heal the organization's ills. Action research process consultation logics have dominated our thinking about how to "do" management consulting, and this mode of thinking is still very prominent today in management consulting education and in practice at places like Deloitte, Accenture, the Boston Consulting Group, and the myriad big-shop and boutique consulting firms that permeate the landscape of management consulting today. Susan was trained in action research methods at Deloitte, although it was called something else to brand it in the Deloitte way, which is commonly done across the management consulting industry.

In recent years, a new process model has come on the scene that challenges the problem-centric approach of action research. Stimulated by the growth in positive psychology, and its manifestation in positive organizational scholarship in the field of management, opportunity-centric methods are now being used by many consultants. The most commonly known positive approach is called appreciative inquiry, and it was invented by David Cooperrider and associates at Case Western University. Those who study and apply appreciative inquiry methods believe that problem-centric approaches can increase skepticism toward the consultant, bog the process down in negativity, and distract the process from more efficiently and effectively achieving its ends. Appreciative inquiry represents an alternative to action research with emerging new methodologies that elevate individual and organizational strengths, and where normative existence within the organization is shifted toward the exceptional or extraordinary (Cooperrider, 1990; Cooperrider and Avital, 2004; Cooperrider, Whitney, and Stavros, 2003; Ludema, Whitney, Mohr, and Griffin, 2003; Whitney and Trosten-Bloom, 2003). I should also note that I introduced this method to the field of community psychology, with David Bright, who worked with David Cooperrider and colleagues during his doctoral studies at Case Western, as a way for community psychologists to enhance the long tradition of participatory action research in community scholarship and consulting (see Boyd and Bright, 2007). That effort was another example of scholarship at the intersection of organization studies and community psychology and, in this case, was an importation and adaptation of management advances to the field of community psychology.

Appreciative inquiry as an opportunity-centric change methodology has progressively gained stature as a viable and effective organization development strategy. During the past couple of decades, scholars and practitioners have honed a method that creates an atmosphere for opportunity-centered change into a practitioner model known as the 4-D cycle: Discover, Dream, Design, Destiny (see Table 4.1; Cooperrider et al., 2003; Ludema et al., 2003; Whitney et al., 2002).

Discover. The underlying assumption of the Discover phase is that people enact intrinsically held assumptions and images into the reality of organizational life (Cooperrider, 1990). Created by the social constructions of language and stories, these assumptions and images generally lead to events and actions that reinforce the way members speak and think about the organization. Positive images refer to an ideal state about what should be in organization practice: how people should treat one another and what the organization should represent or strive for. The primary goal is to create an awareness of images, stories, and capacities that are most likely to inspire future organizing. A well-executed opening activity uses questions to generate an atmosphere of energy, focus, and anticipation for alternative possibilities and assumptions. The Discover phase initiates intentional conversations among organization or system members, often involving hundreds of participants.

Dream. The Dream phase alters the focus of inquiry from discovering existent strengths to a consideration of how these strengths can be leveraged (Bright, Cooperrider, and Galloway, 2006). The key question is "What could be . . .?" The dialogue in this phase is practical: It is based on the organization's history, and it allows for an expansion of thinking about an organization's potential. The themes from the previous phase are used to design and expand aspirations for change, challenging the status quo and building synergy. Events generate an atmosphere of playfulness and creativity. Participants might work in groups to create artwork, poetry, or a skit to depict an ideal future, where the highest dreams, passions, and aspirations become clearly apparent. Participants might also summarize and prioritize key themes or ideas for action. In sum, the Dream phase draws on the best of the past and present in a way that maximizes the capability for expansive thinking about the potential future.

Design. The Design phase initiates a shift from reflection to action. The major task is to identify concrete, actionable ideas that will move the organization closer to its newly envisioned potential. A key task is the formation of action groups, organized to focus on the implementation of prioritized ideas and to operationalize dreaming. Team development activities aim to build strong, focused teams with a clear sense of purpose and identity. Groups generate a statement of aspirations and develop a plan to enact these aspirations. Because people are more likely to become actively engaged in a particular initiative when they are involved from inception to implementation (Burke, 2002), self-organization and self-governance are prominent. Participants are free to choose or propose any group based on common interests. In the ideal scenario, emergent leaders become actively engaged in planning change, fostering an atmosphere of commitment and purpose, a sense responsibility that encourages supportive behaviors, the enhancement of innovation and creativity, and the opportunity for skill development in leadership (Harrison and Freeman, 2004).

Destiny. The Destiny phase is a transition from planning to deployment as teams implement their plans to create change. Each plan might include refined aspirations, goals, major milestones, and an assignment of team leadership. It might include discussions about how often to schedule team meetings, how final decisions will be made, or how to stay connected through virtual technologies. As in any change event, the key is to create a plan for perpetuating the momentum from the planning stages to reality as people return to their day-to-day responsibilities. Destiny's most obvious effects are found in the degree to which teams carry out their plans.

Susan shares all of this information with Amanda and her leadership team during their next meeting, and she adds that some new process advances have come on board while she was at Deloitte in the last 10 years. One of them is Design Thinking. As Plattner, Meinel, and Leifer (2011) explain, design thinking is a five-stage process that includes (1) (re)defining the problem, (2) needfinding and benchmarking, (3) ideating, (4) building, and (5) testing. Originally emanating from fields like engineering, architecture, industrial design, and product and systems design, and evidenced in places like Stanford's Design School (D-School), "design thinking" is a process, a set of skills, and a mindset. And, it has spread across academic disciplines and found a home in management consulting. Another innovation is Agile (Harvard Business Review, 2020), which is a mindset and method for improving innovation through customer collaborations that employ adaptive testing and learning. Agile teams are typically small cross-functional groups dedicated to studying organizational processes, improving customer products and services, and evaluating the technologies that enable strategy, structure, and process. Each team typically has an "owner" (someone responsible for the team) and a "coach" (someone who mentors a team), and team members break down complex issues into manageable chunks where they work on solutions in that particular module. Modules are executed in short cycles (usually less than a month) in what are called "sprints." Team members hold daily "stand-up" meetings to resolve issues and keep everyone on track, and they continuously test ideas and prototypes in concert with the client.

After reviewing various process consultation methods, Susan explains to the leadership team that they will need to define a specific process model or create a hybrid model that infuses elements of various techniques. She also mentions that it would be a good idea to create a steering committee for the project that is based on stakeholder representation, instead of the project solely emanating out of the leadership group. There are some hesitations to that suggestion, but after a few back-and-forth exchanges, the group agrees to go with the steering committee idea. They spend the rest of their time defining various stakeholders, and they ultimately agree that Susan, Amanda, a couple of leadership team members (Sarah the HR VP and Linda the CFO), three midlevel managers and three employees from different departments, and two members of the board should join the committee. Susan helps to refine this list and is cognizant of the fact that the group should have more staff members than upper leadership in their ranks to help empower employees and avoid perceptions that management will control the process. They also agree that they would like to start the process by infusing some appreciative inquiry logic into their call for committee members. The next day, the following letter goes out to all of the employees and the board members of the organization:

Dear Members of our Community:
As you all know, Sarah Gleitner (VP of HR) recently led an effort to stimulate discussions with managers across the organization to learn what we are doing well and how we can improve. I know that we have not done this before, and I also know that there is likely skepticism about our honest intent to listen to you and to try and improve our community. In an effort to move forward in good faith, I have enlisted the services of Susan Kendrick, the CEO and principal consultant from Excite Consulting. Susan has a decade of management consulting experience with Deloitte Consulting and Excite, and she has already helped the leadership team learn that we can do a better job of listening to you and using your insights to help us build a thriving community. With that in mind, we would like to form a steering committee that will be composed of six employees (which will be a majority of the group), and in addition, will include stakeholders from the board of directors, the leadership team, and Susan. We would like to design a majority of employees in the group to reduce structural inequities that can occur when leadership and management outnumber others in a decision-making effort. Tomorrow, Sarah Gleitner will send you a Google Form asking for nominations (including self-nominations). We will accept nominations for the remainder of the week to give you a chance to ask questions of your managers and the leadership team. Both groups are ready to fill you in with anything that you might inquire about. Early next week, we will review the nominations, and we anticipate using a lottery (for equal access) with a goal of selecting six members from different parts of the organization (for a wider set of worldviews). Also, you should know that all of the engagement on the steering committee (and future events along the way) will take place during normal business hours, and everything you do will be compensated as part of your regular work. I look forward to your nominations, and I genuinely look forward to working with you as we dream and design a place that we all want to thrive in.

With appreciation for all that is and all that can be,
Amanda

Notice that the appreciative inquiry approach was embedded in the call for nominations by using a positive tone and using keywords like "doing well, thriving, dream, design," and others. In addition, notice that the letter represents an attempt to create inclusiveness for all members of the organization. Community psychologists also value this approach, and it is clear that a hallmark of community psychology is its holistic and ecological perspective of valuing diversity and inclusion in the context of community (Trickett, 1996, 2009). A recent article by Fujimoto, Azmat, and Subramaniam (2019) echoed the sentiments of Trickett during a study of one of the largest pulp and paper companies in the world. They extended the literature on workforce diversity/inclusion by developing the community-inclusive organizational framework, which signifies the dynamics of community inclusiveness of organizations, highlighting key managerial accountabilities (i.e., cultural, collective, relational, and structural accountabilities) based on a community psychology perspective. In line with this work, the letter was designed to show that the leadership of the organization recognizes that structural inequities could exist if there were a greater number of executives and managers in the steering committee. The statements that Sarah and Susan created were also intentionally designed for the purpose of setting a positive direction of the change process. Future communications contained similar positive-oriented and inclusive statements.

Two weeks later, the steering committee met for the first time, and Susan facilitated the meeting. As she had done for the leadership team, she reviewed management consulting process models, and using techniques like storytelling, brainstorming, and individual reflection, the committee decided to combine an action research process with elements of appreciative inquiry (especially dreaming and visioning of the future), and they decided that some design thinking and Agile sprints would be useful as part of the process too. In follow-up sessions over the next two weeks, she taught the committee that management consultants use process models, but they also use content models to guide their work. She reviewed the data that were collected a few weeks back by Sarah in HR, and she noted how most of the feedback related to resources that employees needed or to relationships that they were experiencing at work. Because these data were clearly centered on the culture of the organization, she felt that the community experience model would be a useful content model to guide their inquiry. She trained the group on how to understand the community experience model, and how to ground qualitative and quantitative data collection methods in the theory and logic of the model. Finally, she urged the group to design a mixed-methods study (i.e., qualitative and quantitative), and use that as a primary diagnostic method and way of "discovering" what is going well, and not so well, in relation to the community culture in the firm.

Understanding the Issues and Discovering What's Going On

The mixed-methods study involved two major rounds of data collection. The first round included a qualitative study that was aimed at discovering meanings of community, the importance of community, and major factors that seem to drive community at work.[1] The second round was planned for execution as a sequential quantitative follow-up to the qualitative study because the group believed data from the first study could inform specific measures and hypotheses that could be tested.

The qualitative study involved interviews with the leadership team and upper management, and focus groups with midlevel managers, supervisors, and employees. Interviews were used for top leadership because the group was relatively small and accessible (i.e., the sampling frame was small enough to allow for it), and focus groups were used with managers, supervisors, and employees who were more numerous. Each interview focused on characterizing how senior leaders define the culture of the community, how they believe community develops, and what types of outcomes occur as a function of community experiences at work. At the outset of the interview, Susan (or one member from the steering committee) stated the following:

> As we start the conversation today, we would like to orient you to the operational definition of "community experience" that we will be using. A community experience is your perception of feeling like you are part of a community when you go to work. An experience that is present within the organization, your work unit, the office when you are at work.

The following questions were asked in succession during the interview:

1) When you think of having an experience of community at work, what does that mean to you? What are the elements of a community experience?
2) Do you have experiences of community at work, and how are they manifested?
3) What are the factors or conditions that foster a sense of community at work?
4) What are the factors that reduce a sense of community at work?
5) When a sense of community is present, what do you think it leads to at the organization level? At the work unit level? At the customer level? At the individual employee level? At the external community level?
6) Before we conclude, is there anything that you would like to ask or comment on?

1. Portions of this section were previously published in N. Boyd and S. Larson (2023). Building community at work: An exploratory study in healthcare system management. *Journal of Community Psychology*, *51*(5), 2276–2299.

Next, focus groups were conducted with midlevel managers, supervisors, and employees. Questions were identical to those used in interviews with upper management. Focus groups were conducted for approximately 90 minutes, and they included 7–10 individuals in each session. All focus groups were conducted by Susan, and one member from the steering committee was present to assist with notes on flip charts and to record the session.

Interviews and focus groups were transcribed by associates at Susan's firm, and steering committee members and Susan independently reviewed them and developed coding schemes for content analysis of the data. They followed guidelines for qualitative analysis rigor where the coding scheme was developed in an interpretivist tradition, in that they were not specifically intending to test hypotheses. Instead, they formulated expectations of the findings relative to the community experience model, and the expectations guided the qualitative analysis for the purpose of theory building (see commentaries about qualitative research in community psychology—Banyard and Miller, 1998; Nelson and Evans, 2014; Stewart, 2000; and management—Gummesson, 2000).

Results of the Qualitative Study

Once the data were ready, the steering committee convened to review the information and plan for next steps. The findings across the various subject groups were remarkably similar, although at times, specific responses were a function of one's vantage point. Here is what they found.

Community Matters

At some point during every session, whether stimulated by the investigators via a probing question or unsolicited by respondents, individuals unequivocally reported that community experiences matter. Respondents felt that they wanted to work in settings where they personally experienced community, they believed it should be a focus of administrators, and they collectively noted that it should be cultivated throughout the system. As one manager put it, "it's fundamental to our existence."

The Elements of Community Experiences

When asked to consider what a community experience at work means, and to highlight its components, responses were remarkably similar to the constructs of a sense of community (and its subelements) and a sense of community responsibility. Respondents consistently mentioned that they experience community when they feel like they are part of a group (membership), when they have a say in what goes on (influence), when they feel bonded to others (shared emotional connections), and when their basic needs and needs for affiliation are met (need fulfillment). Many individuals also mentioned that they experience community during acts of service toward others, which is consistent with the notion of a sense of community responsibility. One midlevel manager said, "I think our highest customer satisfaction is in our customer care unit, and they are at 98–99 percentile ranking because they work as a family and a community."

Multilevel Outcomes of Community Experiences

When asked why community experiences matter, the data revealed that responses can be organized in concert with multilevel impacts as expressed in the community experience model. Respondents felt that community experiences lead to impacts for individuals, units where people work, the entire company, and even beyond the boundary of the organization to external settings.

Individuals. Many employees felt that they would be happier, content, and satisfied with their jobs if they felt a sense of community. These types of statements are consistent with propositions that a sense of community should help improve psychological well-being outcomes for employees. Moreover, a variety of respondents indicated that a sense of community responsibility has implications for individual employees. One manager stated, "there is intrinsic reward . . . at the staff level who stay, because there is higher sense of enjoying that you found something that you think is meaningful and has purpose for others." Employees also shared that effort, productivity, quality of work, intention to stay, resilience, and ownership would occur for those who experience community at work.

Work Unit. A variety of outcomes were expressed for work units within the organization. Most commonly, people believed that unit productivity would rise, and that efficiency, quality, and customer satisfaction would increase. Put simply by one respondent, "the customer experience is driven by employee engagement." Others shared sentiments like "we are never going to be successful in my unit unless we are happy, and this company has never been really good at worrying about our happiness, and getting us to feel like a community." Also, a common narrative emerged around creating an annual employee engagement survey and that including measures of community experiences would be useful. Some said that if an engagement survey existed, they would bet that work unit data would be critical. One senior executive aptly put it by stating, "when I think about survey results [on employee satisfaction], I would especially like to see the relationship with unit leaders." In addition, a variety of respondents reported that community experiences directly relate to quality satisfaction metrics, greater retention, fewer job vacancy rates, less negative chatter, and an abundance of social rewards in the unit.

The Organization. Many of the reported outcomes for the organization mirrored findings at the work unit. Respondents noted that productivity, efficiency, quality, safety, customer satisfaction, retention, and organizational performance would all result from greater community experiences within the workforce. As one executive stated, the bottom line is "we're going to go about this to create the best place to work, and the best place to serve customers, therefore the best financial outcomes." Collectively, many individuals believed that financial sustainability and market share would improve as a function of greater community experiences at work.

The External Community. Respondents signaled that the path to financial sustainability and market share would mostly be a function of positive stories and brand images that were spread into the external community by customers, staff, executives, and other stakeholders. One person put it like this: "I've been to BBQ's and baby showers, and people that you know who work for the company get talking, and there is a lot of passion about being roughed up." This particular individual was talking about negative perceptions of employees who were feeling "beat up" by the lack of community at work, and the implications of consistent images like this in the local community. A variety of respondents noted that persistence of negative stories spread like a virus, and of course, it would be preferable for employees and the organization if positive stories pervaded the public discourse. For example, a manager shared the following story: "My husband was visiting me at work, and it was his birthday, and some of employees saw it was his birthday, and they made sure to say 'happy birthday,' and they sang to him. I'll never forget that." Many respondents noted that positive word-of-mouth stories would have impacts in the local community, and as far across the globe as stories can travel. The most common response besides brand reputation was that employees would more likely engage in their local communities if they experienced community at work. One person described "a sense of community, and a pride to even wear it outside in the community versus to put it in my pocket because I'm going to the store." This comment is intriguing, because the respondent was saying that their social identity manifests partly because of their affiliation with the company, and if the system lacked community experiences, they would be embarrassed to disclose their organizational affiliation in public. On the other hand, many individuals shared that engagement in the local community increases when they experience community within the company. Respondents stated,

> You do feel you have a sense that you want to represent the company . . . by getting involved, whether it's in school boards or local bank boards or volunteering, and because of a sense of community, we've got folks representing us at walks and runs, and dinners, as coaches, and all kinds of things.

Building Community Experiences

The qualitative study also explored factors that lead to the development of a sense of community and a sense of community responsibility at work. The content analysis that Susan and others conducted revealed a series of themes, or conceptual areas, where antecedents existed. These included corporate-suite (C-suite) leadership support of the organization as a community, broad organizational context features, organizational structure, HR issues, the work unit, and job and individual characteristics.

C-Suite Leadership Support of the Organization as a Community. Respondents noted that the corporate suite is especially responsible for setting a tone toward creating community experiences. Many individuals suggested that executive leadership needs to intentionally focus on a concept of community, create a messaging strategy, and articulate verbal and nonverbal messages across the system (see Table 4.2). As one executive stated, "If you're the leader, it's trying to get people to work together for that common goal of community . . . it starts at the top of the organization because that sets a tone." Once the concept of community is created, and a messaging strategy is designed and executed, respondents especially noted that it is crucial to test the efficacy of the messaging and determine whether accurate transfer of messaging is occurring throughout the system. As one executive put it, "as it gets filtered down to the lowest level, the message isn't delivered in the same context." Respondents also consistently stated that top executives need to model community behavior within the C-suite and as part of their daily identity. They should be friendly, accessible, good listeners, and consistently demonstrating that community experiences at work are important. A manager expressed this succinctly, "Modeling is the key . . . as is transparency and communication about community, and not just asking me to do something, but helping me understand why it's important."

Beyond a focus on community and a messaging strategy, many individuals expressed that the C-suite plays an integral role during an implementation phase. They argued that top executives need to be visible and spend as much time as possible on the floor with staff to model behaviors of community experiences. Many respondents shared that Amanda is not especially visible, and they feel that a trend of micromanagement has pervaded the system for years, which facilitated a culture of action by fear. Instead, they strongly suggested

Table 4.2 C-SUITE LEADERSHIP SUPPORT OF THE ORGANIZATION AS A COMMUNITY

Concept and Messaging
CEO support for the organization as a community
CEO and leadership messaging/support on community in the organization
A mission of community versus a financial performance mission
Brand image of the organization that is community oriented
Accurate transfer of communication messages about community throughout the system
CEO expectations of community-like behavior
CEO and C-suite modeling community-like behaviors
CEO and leadership visibility on the floor
Community within the C-suite
Team cohesion in the C-suite
Executive team that collaborates effectively
Open communication encouraged and supported in the C-suite
Greater access to the CEO and CEO responsiveness
Implementation
Organizational commitment to create supportive environment for employees
Decentralization management approach—delegation more than micromanagement
Decentralization of meetings
Leadership knowing many employees
Top management rewarding other managers for strong employee satisfaction

that Amanda and top executives needed to celebrate the successes of decentralized individuals and units who were achieving cultures of community. Relatedly, they expressed that executive leaders need to design decentralization and delegation schemes and build an infrastructure that rewards managers for the creation and maintenance of community cultures in their units. As one respondent noted, "If you engage them, they'll learn faster than if you just tell them . . . and people will take initiative to innovate cultures of community."

Organizational Structure and Context. Respondents also expressed that the evolution of the company over time has impacted community experiences (see Table 4.3). Over the past several years, the company has grown considerably, and respondents argued that size and hierarchy have reduced community experiences. One individual noted, "we used to be a lot smaller, and there was a true sense of the workforce being a community because we were small."

Finally, respondents signaled that two additional factors were important in the context of attempting to create community experiences at work. They

Table 4.3 ORGANIZATIONAL STRUCTURE AND CONTEXT

- Size and hierarchy
  - Stronger sense of community when organization is small
  - Identity of town and organization are synonymous in terms of their identity.
    - Everyone used to know everyone.
    - Percentage of employees that come from the local area
    - Multigenerational continuity in the organization
  - Too many hierarchical layers and too much bureaucracy
  - Problem of silos
  - Running the organization as disjointed units
- Financial issues
  - Budget constraints and performance of the organization
  - Financially driven goal priorities are a problem.

noted that a focus on financial performance has always permeated the company, and that many individuals were experiencing fear and pressure to deliver financial results. Some felt that it was like a dark cloud consistently hovering over their heads, and they resented the fact that fast expansion had contributed to some of the financial woes.

Characteristics of Connection in Work Units. The findings clearly revealed that the executive leadership plays an important role in defining and facilitating community at work; however, respondents consistently and strongly argued that people and activity in the work units are central to delivering the goods (see Table 4.4). Many respondents said that it is critical for community experiences to develop within a work unit, near the epicenter of individual psychological experiences at work. One of the most persistent findings was that employees crave connection with others. And, that can happen in a myriad of ways. One respondent noted, "I think the greatest sense of community is work group specific, but when I look at them, I can almost say, that group's tighter knit, and I know why, it's because they socialize outside of work." Perhaps the most poignant statement about connection with others was offered by a manager who said, "I need to have a friend, at least one, in my work unit. Someone I can vent to and share my life with." Respondents noted a number of impediments that get in the way of being able to deeply share their lives with others. They said their workdays were overscheduled and they were stretched too thin with task demands. One person lamented that "watercooler time" has essentially vanished, and that the drive toward operational efficiency and financial performance had eroded the normalcy of human

Table 4.4 CHARACTERISTICS OF CONNECTION

Sense is of community is more likely to occur at individual unit level.

Sources of connection

- Socializing and personal relationships outside of work
    - Running into other employees in public space
    - Locality of employee (if they live close)
    - Other local connections (family members, etc.)
- Friends in the office
- Sharing personal aspects of your life with others
- Social gatherings (holiday parties, picnics, etc.)
- Amount of time spent together
- Physical proximity and face-to-face time
- Open space in the schedule. Opportunities to commune with others.
    - Excessive scheduling
    - Hardwiring downtime into the day
    - Being stretched too thin

Characteristics of individuals

- Empathy
- Extroverts
- Optimistic people
- Nice people
- Environment where there are a lot of outwardly caring people
- Environment that supports emotional expression
- Leave ego at the door
- Altruistic versus personal gain
- Sense of social responsibility
- How I view the institution's purpose
- Aspiration to be something greater that they currently are
- High expectations of themselves/perception that they want to do a great job
- Me as an individual feeling like I'm on a mission

interaction. Others regretted the cancellation or modification of holiday parties, and other small and large organizational social gatherings. An employee stated it like this: "Oh, I really miss the company picnic! We had it out here on the lawn, and we had, you know, our families come. We all kind of got together, we did caricatures and such, but we don't do that anymore and that hurts. " A few senior executives shared that ramping up weekly meetings and monthly conference calls were important interventions to keep in touch with employees, but on the whole, employees wanted to enjoy the simpler things in life. They wanted to spend time together.

Respondents also felt that characteristics of individuals were important. One employee shared that "you need at least one social butterfly in the unit." Many individuals noted that you need people to stimulate community experiences through extroversion, empathy, optimism, and kindness. When you have individuals who embody these characteristics, people are more likely to be drawn together, and as one person put it, "you are able to celebrate the small things, like birthdays, weddings, births of children, winning a Little League championship, and so on." Such individuals were also thought to act as a spark to stimulate condolences for a lost family member, the passing of a family pet, the lack of a child's acceptance into their dream college, and the myriad of life's challenges when people need emotional support. Many reported a desire to work in environments where manifestations of caring people were common, and they aspired to work in a setting where emotional expression was normalized.

Respondents also expressed that "other-regarding" attitudes and behaviors were important for stimulating a sense of community responsibility. One person opined about the need for employees to "leave their egos at the door," while another said, "it's nice when workers are focused on responsibility to others and not so focused on what they can get." In a related way, several individuals shared that a key ingredient to community experiences is hiring individuals who are on a mission, who have high expectations for themselves, and at the same time, who aspire to help themselves and others around them be something greater than they currently are. This point could be summarized as a set of individuals who are interested in "lifting all boats" instead of merely focusing on themselves.

Managerial Characteristics. It was also evident that one of the most important individuals for creating a culture of community was the manager of the unit (see Table 4.5). Many respondents referred to the logic and need for social butterflies and responsible actors, but they persisted in a desire for the unit leader to embrace these human characteristics. They reported that it is critical for a manager to be visible, accessible, open minded, caring, and responsible. As one person put it, "employees need to see their leader as a human, not just someone telling them what to do, and that you are vested in their benefit by helping them." Another noted, "There were two employees waiting by the front door, and they were talking about how bad their day was and their supervisor doesn't listen, and they talked to him, and he didn't do anything and one was crying." Respondents expressed a desire for managers to stimulate cultures of community through a variety of simple human attributes, and to creatively design mechanisms to foster community. Some of the interventions included coffeehouse talks, open forums, organizing social events, socially rewarding employee achievements, and constantly messaging in public, "How can I help you?" The point here is that no single intervention is a silver bullet, but instead through a mixture of being a "good" human being,

Table 4.5 MANAGERIAL CHARACTERISTICS

Facilitators

- Leaders needs to be accessible and visible.
- Managers/supervisors who encourage input from employees
- Managers saying "thank you, you've done a great job"
- Have leaders celebrate the small things.
- Managers who are open minded, patient, and supportive
  - Good communication, fairness, transparency, authenticity, concern
  - Need to know that they can go to a trusted channel to communicate
  - Genuinely supportive
- Helping people realize their dreams
- Asking employees to share their aspirations at work and in life
- Managers and employees who actively engage in conflict resolution
- Honest and critical feedback
- Open communication between employees, managers, etc.
  - Casual communication (coffeehouse talks) with managers
  - Communication in a team-based oriented way
  - Knowing that it's okay to talk about things other than work
  - Capability to speak up and be heard
  - Consistent open forums with staff—miniforums to work on staff engagement
- Do you have everything you need to get your job done? (resources and info)
  - Managers and leaders doing their work for the common good of the team—not about them

Impediments

- Being disrespected by leadership or management
- Not listening to employees as individuals
- Middle managers who get in the way of messages about the sense of community
- Leaders who feel they can't change anything are a problem.

and creatively designing "community interventions," there is a greater probability of stimulating community experiences at the epicenter where employees work.

Job and Other Work Unit Characteristics. Beyond the role of the manager, several additional factors were highlighted as important ingredients within jobs and features of a work unit (see Table 4.6). Several respondents expressed that job levels and job types impact community experiences. One manager stated, "I work with employees in accounting. They're in an office, and they don't interface with our customers, so they don't really have that sense of why they do what they do and how does that contribute." Respondents also

Table 4.6 JOB AND WORK UNIT CHARACTERISTICS

Job characteristics	
	Job level, type of job, and type of unit
	Relationship between higher level and lower level employees
	Lack of clarity of job title
	Continuity of a work team over time
Features in the context of a work unit	
	Similarity of values, behaviors, and appearance of workers
	Similarity in work ethic
	Similarity of age breeds similarity on numerous things (experience, kids, etc.)
	Generational differences (millennials vs. baby boomers, etc.)
	How long specific individuals have been a member of the work unit around the respondent

frequently referred to an "us versus them" mentality when it came to certain employee interactions like "management versus employees," and that hierarchy in job roles can be a detriment to community experiences. On the flip side, there were consistent and strong messages that managers and leaders need to play a role in dissuading these arbitrary role barriers. One executive expressed it eloquently by saying,

> I had a meeting the other day and I made the mistake of saying that that some of my employees don't serve customers, and one of the employees called me out. I felt stupid . . . I felt like I blundered badly, but later that week, I shifted my tone and gave a speech about a facilities worker who had passed away tragically, and how important they were to delivering customer care. I learned an important lesson that we all play a part in community.

Respondents also expressed a number of interesting contextual features that could influence the development of community experiences. A major theme emerged on a dialectic of homogeneity versus heterogeneity in values, behaviors, and attitudes. In general, respondents believed that similarity generated greater community experiences. They believed that similarity in age, work and life experiences, value stances, and other demographic similarities could foster in-group community experiences. These comments provide a challenge in the growing diversification of a workforce and calls for diversity and inclusion, but as one respondent put it, "even though employees might not be the same, we need to find ways to help them see that they have common values and goals." Relatedly, several individuals noted that the longer employees work together, the greater the chance that they will find, or managers can help them find, common points of connection.

Human Resource Management

The final area that respondents discussed was the importance of human resource management in advocating and designing systems to stimulate community at work (see Table 4.7). Many individuals expressed that the VP of human resources should take a lead in calling for community constructs to be embedded within the culture of the organization and across all HR systems. Beyond the need for basic hygiene features of employment (e.g., job security, adequate compensation and benefits, hiring/budget freezes, salary cuts), respondents articulated that community concepts need to be included in job analysis and job descriptions. They also believed that managers should hire individuals who want to be a part of a community, and who desire to have responsibility for their work, their coworkers, and the organization.

One manager put it like this: "We traditionally don't hire anybody on anything other than do you have the skills needed. Shouldn't we be hiring people who want to join a community and take care of it?" Many individuals expressed that training and development should start with onboarding where new employees are introduced to the importance of community and how to contribute toward it. Training should continue throughout the career of an employee, and respondents especially pointed at the need for managerial training and organization development on community experiences. One executive noted that managers are often promoted without the requisite skills in relation to community by stating, "You make somebody chair of a department and, they are great doctors and surgeons and good at patient care, but are they leaders in developing communities?" Many respondents noted the importance of good compensation and benefits, but they also believed compensation schemes should be directly linked to community experiences. One way to achieve this is through the development and inclusion of more group reward systems, and incentive systems that help improve community experience behaviors for employees and managers.

Respondents stated that HR could lead a variety of employee relations interventions. They also expressed that HR should take a role in keeping the annual picnic and perhaps they should add an employee recognition dinner. Like previous findings mentioned earlier, people were fearful that social gatherings could become a thing of the past. Several respondents mentioned that events like these are important for members of the leadership to show how much they care about the community at work, especially when they greet employees at the door, serve meals, and let their guard down and act like human beings. Similar to employee and managerial accountabilities noted earlier, many respondents expressed that community experiences should be included in annual employee performance appraisals, and HR scorecards with key performance indicators (KPIs) of community should be shared within work units

Table 4.7 HUMAN RESOURCE MANAGEMENT

Job analysis/job descriptions	
	Embed community concepts in job analysis and job descriptions
Recruiting/hiring/job descriptions	
	Hiring people with a sense of community responsibility
	Hiring those who value teamwork and people wanting to be part of a community
	Hiring or budget freezes
Training	
	Merit-based for training opportunities, promotion opportunities, career development
	Onboarding program that focuses on community at work and becoming a member of it
	Training managers on aspects of community so they can develop it in their work units
	Career counseling, mentoring, continuing education programs
	Organization development interventions on community
Compensation/benefits	
	Good benefits, compensation (living wage), healthcare benefits
	Public transportation and easy accessibility to get to work
	Bonuses
	Group-based rewards
	Creating incentive programs for employees that align to patient outcomes
	Potential salary cuts
Employee relations	
	Engaging in employee engagement/climate surveys
	Good managerial coaching
	Annual employee recognition dinner
	Venues where everyone gets together socially
	Leaders stand and greet people as they walk in the door, serve meals, etc.
	Job security
Performance appraisal	
	Sharing info, data, and HR scorecards with employees
	Process standards and performance expectations of community
Termination	
	How terminations are carried out (impersonal termination methods)

and across the system. There were also some interesting comments about termination methods and the lack of human connection when someone leaves the system. One executive stated in the case of a recent job cut,

> [T]he person hasn't died, so we should celebrate them, and take it upon ourselves to learn what we didn't know about them. We should take them out as a team to celebrate their life and their contributions and let them know although in 24 hours they will not be with us at work, that we haven't forgotten them, and what they have done as coworkers for us.

These are the types of impersonal actions that a variety of individuals felt were stimulated by rigid HR policy.

PLANNING TO BUILD COMMUNITY

The data from the qualitative study were expansive, detailed, and extremely helpful to the steering committee. They convened at their next meeting to review the data, discuss the implications of its meaning, and plan for next steps. As the meeting commenced, Susan expressed her gratitude for the efforts of committee members in collecting the data and in organizing the content for public dissemination. One of the employees remarked, "It's been a real pleasure. I've never worked at a place where I had a chance to be involved in a project like this from start to finish. Thank you." Others in the room shared similar sentiments, and there was a clear sense of energy in the air. Susan then asked, "So what do you all think we should do next?" An employee suggested they should present the data to the entire organization, and a board member agreed. A supervisor expressed that she believed they had enough data to act now, and there was a robust back and forth about the immediate need for more data versus planning to collect quantitative data in a few months. Amanda chimed in by saying, "This process has been a real eye-opener, and I think we should listen to these data and follow their lead." Susan continued facilitating the meeting, making sure to hear from all of the stakeholders in the room; as they were reaching a point of consensus, she offered the following,

> OK, so it seems like we're starting to coalesce on a strategy of next steps. Based on our hybrid action research/appreciative inquiry consulting process, we just completed a solid diagnosis, and we certainly heard a number of dreams about what a positive future could look like. I think we agree that we have a pretty good content road map on important antecedents that relate to community experiences, and we have a decent idea of what community experiences can produce. I also heard us say that we want to wait in collecting quantitative data, and that we want to do so during our inaugural employee engagement survey in 6–10 months. As the next phase develops we can entertain discussions on a quantitative data collection approach and decide if we would like to use the Brief Sense of Community Scale [BSCS; Peterson, Speer, and McMillan, 2008], the Sense of Community Index II

> [SCI-2; Chavis, Lee, and Acosta, 2008], the Psychological Sense of Community scale [PSCS; Jason, Stevens, and Ram, 2015], or the Sense of Community Responsibility scale [SCRS; Nowell and Boyd, 2014; Treitler, et al., 2018]. Let's type this and other plans into a Google Doc and display it on the screen.

The following is what was produced:

1) Further investigate, via the formation of working groups, how to dream and design future states that facilitate and remove barriers, to community experiences in each of the areas that emanated from the qualitative study.
2) The working groups will coordinate their activity with Susan and the steering committee, and they will use Design Thinking and Agile sprints as techniques to design a positive future state.
3) One working group will work with Susan to design the inaugural employee engagement survey, which will include questions linked to important antecedents, community experience measures (sense of community and sense of community responsibility), and outcomes. The HR folks will help us gather performance data and other individual outcome measures, and we will figure out how to measure and assimilate unit, organizational, and external stakeholder data into the data set so we can run various statistical analyses on the data.
4) The steering committee will hold a town hall meeting within the next 2 weeks with the entire organization to update them on the findings of the qualitative study, share plans for the working groups, and emphasize that we are committed to creating a thriving community.

As the meeting was ending and steering committee members were leaving the room, Amanda approached Susan, and gave her a hug.

> I really want to thank you for everything you've done, Susan. I can't believe how much I've learned from you in such a short period of time, and I am hopeful that our future work will produce exciting results. I really wish I had learned more about this stuff when I was in school, but heck, at least I know better now.

Susan immediately quipped, "I can see that you 'get it,' and nothing could be more satisfying."

CHAPTER 5

Putting It All Together and Building Community

PUTTING IT ALL TOGETHER

The following Sunday afternoon, Amanda and Ken are on a walk in the neighborhood while Amanda's parents are at home watching the kids. Ken is taking pictures of various things, and at one point he stops near the edge of the neighborhood park. "What were you shooting honey?" Amanda asked. "Oh, I was trying to get a shot of the juxtaposition between the landscape in the park and the adjacent property. The contrast between the manicured lawn and some of the new natural and native species landscaping in the park is interesting." Amanda loves that about Ken. He sees things that she can't see, and he reminds her that new lenses on issues are normal and often better than the way others see them. That's not to say that she always agrees with his vision on everything, but she loves him for who he is, and how he views the world. The past month at work has been a similar journey for Amanda, as Susan has helped her to see a new way forward in running her company: a future where organizational culture takes center stage, and where nurturing it is becoming a more normalized activity in the firm. "So, honey, what do you think about our conversation yesterday on getting a dog?" asked Ken. Amanda replied,

> Oh, it's funny you say that; I was thinking to myself earlier this morning, that a few months ago, I probably would have said something like, "Well, if you can do most of the work, I'll agree to it," but you know what, why should I say that? I need to let go of my reservations, and my hesitations, and just say yes every once and a while. Let's do it!

Ken immediately exclaimed,

Building Community at Work. Neil Boyd, Oxford University Press. © Oxford University Press (2025).
DOI: 10.1093/9780197635964.003.0006

> Oh my gosh, Gabby and Jensen will be so excited! It's been a while since Benny passed, and it hit me so hard that I wondered for a long time if I would ever have the courage to go through that pain again. Having the love of a dog, and then losing him in such a short period of time was devastating. But, I think I'm ready. Are sure you're OK with us searching for a Newfie?

Amanda reached for Ken's hand, and said, "Yes, babe, I'm more than OK with it."

The next morning, Amanda woke up with a greater sense of calm than she had been accustomed to in recent months, and with a different sense of urgency, as she was ready to take on the challenge of the new week. She was scheduled to meet Susan and the steering committee at 9:00 a.m., and she was looking forward to finalizing the design of the town hall meeting that was scheduled for the following Monday. As the meeting commenced, Amanda looked at the group and said, "Good morning, everyone. It's great to see you all here. What did you do this weekend? I hope you had some fun." One by one, committee members talked about things they experienced over the weekend. An employee took her daughter to the zoo, and she was able to see the wonder in the eyes of her child as she saw an elephant in person for the first time. One of the board members played in the finals of a local United States Tennis Association (USTA) team tennis tournament, and a supervisor went fishing with his niece and nephew. "What did you do Susan?" Amanda asked. "Oh, I worked in the garden, and I started a new book that I've been wanted to read. And, my husband made chicken marsala for dinner on Saturday," Susan replied. "Wow, that's great, Yums! All of that sounds wonderful everyone. I'm glad to hear you had a nice weekend, and I hope this week at work and at home is just as fulfilling," proclaimed Amanda. These words were a contrast in approach for Amanda, but with the influence of Susan, and her new mindset on creating community at work, Amanda knew that she wanted to connect more with others and that relationships were just as important, perhaps more important, than merely focusing on the tasks of the group and work-related issues alone.

The meeting then shifted to Susan taking the lead and reviewing where they stood on their plans for the upcoming town hall meeting.

They all agreed that the following should occur:

1) At the beginning of the workday next Monday, everyone in the company will attend the town hall, and we will have remote conference access for those who can't physically be with us.
2) Amanda will start us off and thank everyone for taking the time over the past several weeks to help us understand the importance of organizational culture, and our commitment to designing and sustaining a thriving community at work. She will mention that folks can ask questions as we

proceed, and that we will make time at the end of the session to answer any questions people might have.

3) Amanda will remind the group that we're in this together, and toward that end, after reintroducing the steering committee members, she will cede the lectern, and various committee members will share ideas for a plan moving forward.
4) Jasmine will get us started and announce that the qualitative findings highlighted the importance of community at work. She will display the community experience model and discuss how a sense of community and sense of community responsibility are at the heart of psychological experiences of community. From there, she will walk us through the rest of the model and highlight that we are especially focused on creating community versus a sole focus on the ends it might produce for the company.
5) Fred will speak next, and he will review the "buckets" that were created as a function of the qualitative analysis (i.e., C-Suite Support, Organizational Structure and Context, Characteristics of Connection, Managerial Characteristics, Job and Work Unit Characteristics, and Human Resource Management). He will announce that we plan to create working groups for each of these issues for in-depth study, that working groups will be composed of cross-functional stakeholder members, and that they will make recommendations for action in coordination with the steering committee.
6) Next, Susan will announce that based on the qualitative study findings, and further analysis of the working groups, an employee engagement survey will be designed to measure community experiences, key antecedents that lead to those experiences, and a series of measures that occur as a function of their existence (or absence).
7) Finally, Amanda will return to the lectern, and answer any questions that individuals might have. All of us should be ready to answer questions if needed, and once we have finished the Q&A, we will adjourn the town hall.

As you can see, the town hall meeting was designed in a way that allowed various members of the steering committee to play a central role in communicating with their fellow community members. This egalitarian design is consistent with the concept of "jointness" that can be embedded in a consulting process, which emanates from the field of organization development and change (Cummings and Worley, 2015). Jointness means that the consultant will work hand in hand with the client and will help to facilitate a space where all are welcome, and needed, to help transition an organization, group, or individual from a status quo to movement. In other words, change management processes that are ascribed to jointness should not solely be controlled and run by the consultant and the management of the organization. This is also precisely what Trickett (1996, 2009) was pronouncing for many years, when he stated that community psychology values diversity and inclusion in contexts of community (Trickett, 1996, 2009). As Burton et al. (2007) and Dalton et al. (2007) note, community psychologists value inclusion of relationships by understanding how individuals, both privileged and less privileged, feel, think, and work together toward creating a better community. This symbolizes the joint participatory process of individuals within organizations, and external stakeholders to organizations, for improving community life as a whole (Dalton et al., 2007; Moritsugu, Vera, Wong, and Duffy, 2014; Scott and Wolfe, 2015).

Organizational members throughout the ecological space at work are all important stakeholders to a change effort, and as the community experience model states, a psychological sense of community involves a perception of influence. People desire the ability to shape their environments, and they will dislike change processes that don't give them such an opportunity. The process started by conversations between Susan and Amanda and, in short order, spread to the leadership team. The design of a steering committee with open opportunities for engagement was an important step in creating a sense of jointness and influence. The town hall was also designed so that everyone could be involved. Of course, there will be skeptics in the ranks of the organization, and behind the scenes conversations might not always be positive, but much of that is a natural part of resistance to change. People won't necessarily change until they are cognitively convinced and emotionally ready to change, and they will need to be assisted on how to take the more difficult step of behavioral change. This is true for every single person in the organization, and it presents a significant challenge for the consultant, the leadership, and the steering committee.

The creation of working groups will be an important step in giving people voice and influence on the future direction of the organization. For some organizational members, it will be the first time that they directly engage in the process besides fulfilling the role of a respondent in a focus group or interview. Being a member of a working group will provide greater agency for more people and give them a sense of ownership and control to design and deliver strategies, structures, and processes that can help the organization and its inhabitants. In the meantime, the qualitative data suggested a number of things that should be acted upon immediately. For example, the C-suite has already started messaging about community and bringing the concept into the lexicon of the organization. They should continue implementing messaging strategies, channel delivery, and walk the talk about community at work. Managers will immediately begin holding daily check-ins with groups and individuals on needs, desires, problems, and issues, and beyond collecting that data for the change effort, they will act to help those who are in their purview. The point is that such low-hanging fruit should not wait for additional study when the qualitative data were clear and compelling. Working groups can take up such issues, and they should, but they should also spend considerable time dreaming, designing, and helping to deliver interventions that are more difficult to address by simple behavioral action.

The management will also need to take a step back from desiring "proof" that working group activity will bring desired organizational outcomes that orient to efficiency and effectiveness. Instead, they will need give agency to the working groups, and give them space to conceive critical antecedents and organizational context features that will drive the creation of community at work. And, they will need to trust that when community at work is achieved, the ends will naturally occur. In other words, they will need to trust that the community experience model (and theoretical models of psychological and management science in general) can deliver what it posits. Tests of the outcomes of community experiences will come in the future as the employee engagement survey is designed, and outcome measures are aligned with measures from that survey. Once such measures are in place, leaders, managers, and employees will have a way to feel the pulse of the organization on a more consistent basis, and make adjustments as necessary for individuals, groups, and the organization as a whole. As Susan has stated multiple times to the steering committee, organizations are social constructions that are often designed, intentionally or unintentionally, without full stakeholder input, and we should give people a chance to take a shot at constructing an organization that they believe they can thrive in.

As Fred noted during the town hall meeting, working groups will immediately commence to study antecedent factors in the organizational context that can lead to community at work. In concert with Fred's statement, the next morning, Amanda sent the following email to everyone at the company:

Good morning, everyone,

Thank you for taking the time yesterday to attend the townhall meeting, and for all you have done so far to help us learn and act in ways that can produce a thriving community at work. As Fred mentioned yesterday, we will immediately commence a series of working groups to further study, dream, and design strategies, structures, and processes that will help us achieve that goal. We plan to create working groups based on the major themes that were generated in the qualitative study we executed over the past month, and various steering committee members will take the lead to get them off the ground. They include:

C-Suite Support (Jasmine Okinwa)
Organizational Structure and Context (Fred Smith)
Characteristics of Connection (Perry Johnson)
Managerial Characteristics (Cassidy Denison)
Job and Work Unit Characteristics (Heather Nguyen)
Human Resource Management (Bill Conners)

Attached below is a summary of the findings in each of these areas for your reference. It is important to note that members of the leadership team will NOT lead the working groups but will instead disperse across the groups as contributors. We want YOU to lead these efforts to help us design a future that YOU want. Like our recent qualitative study, all of the time and energy of the working groups will be conducted during normal business hours at specified times during the next few weeks. We hope to conclude this phase of our work within the next two months. Please click the link below to nominate (or self-nominate) individuals to comprise the working groups. Managers and supervisors at all levels of the organization will assist in this process with an expectation that we will populate the working groups with cross-functional stakeholder members by the end of the week. We plan to kick-off the working groups in 2 weeks. I also want to share that I am 100% committed to this work, and we are in the process of implementing a variety of interventions that can easily be achieved based on the data from the qualitative study. For example, managers and supervisors in your unit will begin holding daily check-ins to listen to your concerns and desires, and they will do their best to help you. Other interventions will be discussed at these check-ins based on recommendations from the steering committee. Please feel free to comment on them and give us feedback if you think there is a way to do it better. We are open to any and all suggestions!

Thank you for listening, and I'm excited about this next phase of our work,

Amanda

Two weeks later, the working groups are populated, and they start by grounding their work in the qualitative data that were recently collected. At this point in a management consulting and change process, Susan is facilitating and monitoring the progress of the groups through their chairs (or cochairs), and she helps them plan for sessions and provides tools that can help them evaluate various topics. For example, the consultant can share process information on how Agile sprints work, how benchmarking across organizational units can be executed, and how data can be analyzed. In the case of Susan, she is also helping to compile information for the working groups and running various analyses to help them progress forward. Without her support, working groups wouldn't be able to advance their work as quickly because everyone in the group has to go back to work after their sessions, and there just aren't enough hours in the day for them to take on the extra burdens of such work.

The first Agile sprint is planned as a 2-week investigation into the data that were collected during the qualitative study. Working groups are charged with reviewing, asking questions, testing new ideas within the group, bouncing them off the steering committee (and Susan), and covering as many issues in their area as possible. At the end of 2 weeks, most groups have covered at least one to three of the major findings in their purview and, when possible, have developed prototypes of what a future state might look like. Their progress after 2 weeks looks like this:

C-Suite Support

Concept and Messaging

> *CEO support and messaging for the organization as a community*
> *Brand image of the organization that is community oriented*

Beyond the work that has already been completed, Amanda and her leadership team are charged with messaging and support in relation to community. From a messaging perspective, the working group recommends incorporating the concept of community in the mission, vision, and values of the firm. Without its presence in these locations, the firm doesn't have a pole star to use a consistent guide in its strategic thinking, and the working group feels this is a critical priority. The group also recommends that the website, print media, and other communication channels need to be reviewed and changed in line with the concept of community being added to the mission, vision, and value statements. For example, the landing page for the retail website and the company website do not currently contain any language or links that relate to community. Their prototypes show specific suggestions for tabs, words, images, and future documents that can help stakeholders easily see that they are committed to building an inclusive community for all stakeholders in the firm. One such document that they envision is an environmental, social, and governance (ESG) report that includes direct information about community in the firm that displays initiatives, metrics, and commitments maintaining a thriving community.

Organizational Structure and Context

- *Size and Hierarchy*
    - *Problem of silos*
- *Financial Issues*
    - *Financially driven goal priorities are a problem*

While the working group acknowledges that steady and incremental growth will be a strategic goal of the firm, they recommend several ideas and prototypes for reducing hierarchy and the problem of departments being disconnected, or siloed, from each other. First, they suggest that Amanda and her leadership team do a better job of communicating with the entire organization about initiatives, policies, and activities that affect people across the firm. Information can get lost in translation, and the previous norm of trickling information from one layer to the next from the top should be redesigned. They suggest several options for this communication strategy, including direct emails from Amanda and key leaders, biweekly mini-town-halls that last approximately an hour, a monthly newsletter, an Intranet location where internal press releases are shared from the major functional units of the organization to keep people up to date, and a Q&A program where employees can ask any question they want and have it answered by the appropriate leadership member or manager via a public outlet (via in-person or electronic means). In relation to financially driven goal priorities, the group suggests that the leadership consider a messaging strategy (on the website, in person, in quarterly investor calls, etc.) that articulates a more sophisticated multiple-bottom-line strategy, which includes financial, environmental, and social constructs. One of their prototypes shows how each of these bottom lines contributes to community, and another one shows how community constructs and metrics are part of a social justice bottom line. Like the previous working group, they suggest creating an environmental, social, and governance reporting (ESG) report, but they believe that a report alone won't achieve the goal of redirecting attention away from a particular focus on the financial bottom line. Instead, they propose a variety of ways that multiple-bottom-line ideation can become normalized in daily activities of the leadership and across the firm that highlight environmental sustainability, social justice, and economic justice (e.g., as part of regular leadership meeting agendas, in every policy change conversation, in public relations press releases, and in "directives" to managers and supervisors for preparation of communications to employees that focus on community)

Characteristics of Connection

Sense of community is more likely to occur at the individual unit level
Sources of Connection
- *Friends in the office*
- *Sharing personal aspects of your life with others*
- *Excessive scheduling*

The characteristics of connection working group focused most of their work on the fact that community experiences are more likely to occur within work units. At face value this made a lot of sense to the group, but they also reviewed recent research studies that corroborated the company's qualitative findings on this issue. They proposed several ideas of how to achieve greater connections with others, including holding short get-togethers where prompts were posed to members of a work unit that allowed them to share about their personal lives. The working group tested this in their own group, and they learned all kinds of things about their members, including who liked soccer, where people went to high school, how they met the loves of their lives, and even that one of their members was fascinated with studying the American Civil War.

That person volunteered to take employees to Gettysburg and spend a day on the battlefield learning about history, and perhaps as equally important, it provided an opportunity for folks to commiserate. The group challenged a prevailing narrative that we should leave our home lives out of work, and that a healthy workplace integrates work as part of a holistic life where work and home life are seamlessly interconnected. They also developed a prototype for what they called "the friend." Using the community experience model as their guide, they showed that friends are people who help their peers feel like a member of the group; fulfill basic, affiliative, and other needs; give space for others to influence the group; and have shared emotional connections with others. Their prototype followed the life cycle of an employee during a typical day and showed how various settings (e.g., parking and arriving, workspaces, meetings, team discussions, etc.) all had the potential for individuals to be influenced by others around them. One of their "deep dives" was around the concept of venting. They proposed that venting is normal, and it shouldn't be construed as inappropriate complaining. And, they showed role players who should be accepting of venting, and what their obligations should be when listening to someone vent (e.g., merely listening, acting on the "vent" by taking it to someone who could fix it, etc.). Another deep dive related to excessive scheduling. They showed a scheduling prototype of an employee who was essentially "booked" the entire day except for a 30-minute period for lunch. They called for action to "humanize" schedules and intentionally plan "refresh bursts" of downtime throughout the day.

Managerial Characteristics

Managers saying "Thank you, you've done a great job," and "Do you have everything you need to get your job done?"
Have leaders celebrate the small things

The managerial characteristics working group spent most of their 2 weeks focusing on some important low-hanging fruit that they believed managers could implement immediately. They signaled that they planned to develop a prototype for a new manager training program that would focus on how leaders, managers, and supervisors can stimulate community as they interact with others in their roles and as individuals; however, they proposed a minitraining that they wanted managers to complete immediately. The training was called "The Simple Things," and it was designed around a phrase that one of the group member's grandmothers always used to say. She was famous in her family for saying things like "It's a simple thing to say 'please and thank you,'" or "How simple was that to ask a question instead of telling your brother he was wrong?" The group argued that the simple ways we interact with our managers and leaders is not an inherent skill, and that data suggested that many of the psychological contract violations in organizations are due to individuals not communicating these simple things. They further suggested that this minitraining be rolled out across the entire organization after a short pilot testing period with managers and leaders. They also developed a checklist for managers and leaders on the kinds of things they need to celebrate, or be concerned about, within their units and in interactions with others. The list included births, birthdays, anniversaries, deaths, injuries, illnesses, graduations, weddings, and a host of others. As part of their simple-things prototype, they articulated that managers need to specifically pay attention to elements of success and pain in the lives of their coworkers, and they need to celebrate, console, and be a point of connection for others. The group mentioned that leaders and managers sometimes need to act like cheerleaders and counselors, and they can't do it at a superficial level. It needs to be genuine, and a required part of the skill set and function of their role.

Job and Work Unit Characteristics

Relationship between higher level and lower level employees
Similarity of age breeds similarity on numerous things (experience, kids, etc.)
Generational differences (millennials vs. baby boomers, etc.)

The job and work unit characteristics group focused on similarity and difference issues and couched much of their work in relation to the community experience model and new information coming from the literature on diversity, equity, and inclusion (DEI) at work. One of their key conclusions was that every single member of the community must experience a sense of mattering and belonging. During the sprint, they read various sections of a new book titled *How People Matter: Why It Affects Health, Happiness, Love, Work, and Society* by community psychologists Issac and Ora Prilleltensky (2021). The authors propose that mattering is a fundamental requirement of human existence, and at its core, people need to feel that others know they exist, that their existence is valued by others, and that others value the contributions that they can bring to the table. Issac Prilleltensky previously noted that mattering consists of *feeling valued* and *adding value* (Prilleltensky, 2014, 2019). He argues that when we feel valued, we are appreciated, respected, and recognized, and feeling valued is a need that can be fulfilled by those around us. When we add value, we are able to contribute to those around us, or to institutions in which we reside. These concepts are well known in community psychology. He further articulates that feeling valued incorporates respect for diversity, the need to belong, inclusion, and fairness. Adding value consists of empowerment, autonomy, a sense of control over our lives, mastery, self-efficacy, and self-determination.

And, it is abundantly clear that many community psychology scholars have produced a literature that expresses the need for sense of community, diversity, inclusion, control, self-efficacy, and empowerment in order to experience wellness (Christens, 2019; Fisher, Sonn, and Bishop, 2002; Nelson and Prilleltensky, 2010; Pretty, Andrews, and Collet, 1994; Pretty et al., 1996; Prezza, Amici, Roberti, and Tedeschi, 2001; Sonn, 2002; Sonn and Fisher, 1996)

Members of the working group discussed that there were many psychological contract violations at work that centered on the concept of mattering. Leaders sometimes felt ignored and slighted, midlevel managers felt that upper management wouldn't take the time to listen to them, and employees regaled the group with stories of how they felt like coworkers and managers didn't recognize their existence in a meeting or a project. The group recognized that an individual doesn't have a chance to "belong" in a group unless mattering is first achieved, and they offered that a focus on mattering would require a review of macro-organizational policies to micro-oriented practices between individuals. They strongly supported the ideas of the other working groups who suggested carving out time for "get-to-know-each-other gatherings" and "the simple things" because their prototypes mirrored those conceptions, but they also suggested a review of organizational policies at the macro level. For example, they highlighted employee handbook policies that contained different vesting timelines and procedures for management compared with employees, and how a call-in/report-off procedure was written in such a way that it only applied to employees, but not the upper ranks of the organization. They called for a review of all policies and procedures that they titled "Resetting and Equalizing the Bar." These types of practices are consistent with "critical" movements in community psychology that have called for a reimagining of the status quo (Angelique et al., 2002) and that give egalitarian power to all participants in a collective setting (Fisher, Sonn, and Evans, 2007; Mannarini, 2012; Sandler, 2007).

They also spent a good amount of time evaluating data and resources around generational, embodied, and other forms of difference, and how the DEI literature can help with interventions that are complementary with the community experience model. For example, community psychologists often look for the impact of culture on the ecologies of communities across multiple levels of analysis (Trickett, 2009). That is, cultural influences permeate across the functioning of individuals and families, organizational practices, and norms of local communities and societies. Thus, the working group could seek an understanding of diverse cultural influences and how company structure and norms, and processes for how decisions are made, how conflict is addressed, and how resources are distributed (Bond and Harrell, 2006).

Kloos et al. (2012) note in their well-regarded community psychology textbook that race, ethnicity, gender, social class, ability/disability, sexual orientation, age, spirituality and religion, and localities (where people are from) are common vantage points in the field of community psychology, although certainly additional categories of DEI can be included in shaping the new culture of the organization.

The working group also noted how psychological experiences are central in various literature streams as a key component of bringing diverse people together, and they especially targeted a prototype that involved a first stage of awareness and understanding about diversity. For example, they urged the organization to run a series of informational sessions, webinars, and other communications that helped people understand all kinds of differences around nuanced questions like "What is Kwanzaa? Do millennials deserve a bad rap? Mansplaining 101? #MeToo involves everyone?" They proposed that the organization take a proactive approach to topics like these as an important step forward in awareness, but also for the sake of publicly signaling that conversations of these types of topics should be part of civic and public discourse at work.

Human Resource Management

Good benefits, compensation (living wage), healthcare benefits
Job Analysis/Job Descriptions
Embed community concepts in job analysis and job descriptions
Hiring those who value teamwork and want to be part of a community
Onboarding program that focuses on community at work
Sharing info, data, and HR scorecards with employees
Performance expectations of community

The HR working group focused on critical resources that employees expect as part of their psychological contract (i.e., excellent wages and benefits), and including community in the organizational context of instrumental HR practice. The group proposed that all employees in the organization deserve at least a living wage, and that common compensation models in the field of HR that benchmark industry wages and salaries with labels like "below market, at market, and above market" should be critically challenged. They argued that investing in people should be a critical priority, which is aligned to the overall strategy of the organization, and they dreamed of a future where wages and benefits worked for, and served, the employee versus merely serving the goals of the organization. For example, they highlighted the story of entry-level employees in their design studio who start at a wage of $54,000 per year, and after detailing typical monthly expenses, cost of living, and the bottom line of monthly take-home wages, it was clear that this job classification was not earning a wage that afforded them much more than a very basic standard of living. Their prototype called for a new way of analyzing compensation beyond mere market-based strategies that have permeated the field of HR for a long time, one that instead looked toward sense-making within the cultural milieu of the organization (Weick, 1995).

They also spent a good deal of time studying and deliberating about a very important HR function called job analysis. Job analysis forms the foundation of many HR functions because at its core, it's about defining the essential job functions of a position. Beyond compliance with employment law, a job analysis defines what a job title will do, and once determined, HR systems like recruiting, hiring, training, compensation, performance appraisal, and more can be aligned to the requirements of a job. The group expressly noted that job analyses for all positions should include, and have accountability for, community at work. Their prototype showed examples of how community constructs would be included in job descriptions, in job ads, on their company jobs portal, in onboarding, and in performance appraisals. For example, the jobs portal (i.e., an HR microsite), included images and language about the importance of community at work, mentioned how all stakeholders are held accountable for community, and provided needed information for prospective employees about the community in the organization and around it. It showed information about the local housing market, schools, recreational activities, restaurants, and more, and every section of the microsite had testimonies and images of current employees that showcased how they experience the local community and the kinds of things they do. It also provided opportunities for prospective employees to connect with current workers to learn more about company culture and the community assets that exist around the organization.

Finally, the HR group discussed and developed a new prototype for annual performance reviews. They showed an approach where new employees receive feedback during their onboarding experience that lasts for their entire first year of employment, and they challenged the current annual performance review system as being dominated by managerial judgment and a lack of buy-in by the employees. Susan shared an article by Boyd and Gessner (2013), which stated that a "just" performance appraisal system requires procedural, distributive, and social justice, and it suggested that performance appraisal systems need to be co-created by various stakeholders in the organization as opposed to its formation by HR or management alone. They mentioned to Susan that such an approach is consistent with how the current consulting process was designed, and is progressing, and they called for a special working group to redesign the system. They mentioned pros and cons with various performance evaluation techniques like graphic rating scales, management by objectives, behavior-based methods, and 360-degree approaches, and they hoped that the special group would work through those issues in their work (DeNisi and Murphy, 2017). They also made a specific point that every single employee should be accountable for the organizational culture and insisted that community measures be included in every performance evaluation. They noted that the leadership team should have their performance tied to company-wide or divisional community measures, that managers at various levels throughout the organization should have specific accountability for creating and excelling at stimulating and managing community within their purview, and that employees should be measured on how they contribute to a thriving community. The group showed that measures like the Brief Sense of Community scale, the Sense of Community Index 2, and the Sense of Community Responsibility scale could be adapted for use in performance reviews. And, they showed how community metrics could be displayed on their website and in various communication channels to both internal and external stakeholders.

BUILDING COMMUNITY

The company was clearly on their way to building community at work, and the next steering committee meeting was full of energy and promise that they were seeing the fruits of their labor. Susan helped them understand that there would be a lot of difficult conversations and decisions in the future. They were still in the midst of appreciative inquiry dreaming and designing, and that would persist for quite some time into the future as actions were pilot tested and ultimately put in place. She was there to help them, but she praised them for all of their progress to date by saying, "You got this. You've been doing a great job so far, and I know you can do it." Amanda chimed in and said, "You know, several months ago, I would have never expected that we would be where we are today, but with the help of Susan, and with our ability to see a new way forward, I'm genuinely excited to see where all of this takes us." They all agreed that creating a community at work was much more complex than they ever would have expected.

The complexity of creating community at work is an interesting artifact in and of itself. Humans appear to be wired in ways that seek simple solutions to problems, and yet we all know that most problems are more complex than we would like. Building community at work will take time, but I also believe that there are several key ingredients to delivering a future where a thriving community exists.

First, like Amanda, individuals need to acknowledge that community is important, and that in the absence of knowing about it, or knowing what to do, one must seek help in the form of consultation, subject matter expertise, and guidance from academic science. I believe that academic science is especially important for two reasons in the present case: (1) to help us understand process models of organization development and change (i.e., action research, appreciative inquiry, Agile, etc.), and (2) to help us understand concepts, models, and theory that form the content by which we can ground our inquiry (i.e., DEI, ESG frameworks, communication methods, strategic planning, HR practices, and many more). Without such guidance, people will often guess at what they should do or quickly turn to easily accessible "best practices," and guessing should not be the main form by which we create and run organizations. The introduction of consultation process models provided a roadmap of where the company was going, and grounding the consulting process in the community experience model provided structure and a rationale of what we should study that were much more advanced than merely "winging it," or seeking a fast solution by copying someone else.

Second, the consultation process, and especially one that is oriented toward creating a thriving community at work, should employ "jointness" or "co-creation" as a central feature. As anthropologists, sociologists, and psychologists would say, cultures are socially constructed (Burr, 2015). And, although some cultures (perhaps too many) are socially constructed by those in power, a thriving community needs to be constructed by all of the stakeholders in the collective. Otherwise, power dynamics will persist and thwart the ability of individuals to feel like they can achieve the concept of influence that is a key component of a sense of community, and top-down cultural design (whether intended or not) will correlate with lessened perceptions and feelings of membership, need fulfillment, emotional connection, and responsibility for the collective. It is imperative that leaders and managers in organizations give employees the ability to co-create with them, and not believe that management has the right to create the organization as they see fit because they "own the firm," or "they are in charge of it." Such worldviews are vestiges of the past, where autocratic management reigned, and 21st-century leaders and managers cannot expect to develop cultures of community if they are unwilling to see new ways of thinking and shed command and control lenses that have permeated organizations for too long (Anderson and Brion, 2014; Christens, 2019).

Third, individuals need to be comfortable with uncertainty and that a process will unfold as it unfolds. Design thinkers and organizational development specialists often use terms like "embracing ambiguity," and "equifinality" as a way to help people understand that there is no specific one best way forward, and that a co-created process will have inherent ambiguity even when specific ends are achieved. Learning to embrace uncertainty is an essential job function of a consultant, but it is also a very important ingredient that will reduce resistance to change in leaders, managers, and employees. Amanda's journey has brought her to a place where the first round of prototypes is being developed, and of course, there is a long road ahead in reaching the ultimate goal of a thriving community at work. The first round covered a small number of low-hanging fruit topics, and future designs will incorporate more topics and more prototypes that relate to community at work. Susan will eventually work with others to design the first employee engagement survey, and quantitative measures of community experiences, organization context variables, and outcome measures for individuals, work units, the organization, and external stakeholders will take shape. Leaders, managers, and employees will evaluate the progress of their designs, and they will embrace the journey as much as the arrival at the destination. Amanda also seems to be incorporating new worldviews at home that were stimulated by the consulting engagement at work, which is a good example of how cultural experiences are able to permeate across the various communities that we inhabit. Like Amanda, all of us have the capacity to conceive, design, and deliver community in our organizations, and in various aspects of our lives, and all it takes is that "first step forward!"

Building Community at Work as Scholars and Practitioners

Building community at work requires us to integrate knowledge and learning from a variety of academic and practice disciplines, and our journey toward building community should give us the freedom to tap into any discipline that can speak to the issues at hand. This book is especially focused on the intersection of community psychology and management to create its main arguments, but as I noted in the introduction, a variety of fields have something to say about conceptualizing and building community at work. Psychological experiences of community are omnipresent in every collective context that we traverse, and therefore I believe the community experience model (Boyd and Nowell, 2014; Nowell and Boyd, 2010) can serve as an excellent guide on a journey toward building community. The knowledge contained in this book about research and analytic tools (qualitative and quantitative), sense of community and sense of community responsibility measures, other constructs about well-being at work, various management consulting process models, and the need to constantly return to academic concepts, models, and theory with an eye on best practices in management and organizational practice give us a path forward in our journey to build community.

Organizational settings dominate our existence, including places where we work, play, and volunteer (Boyd, 2014), and our homes, neighborhoods, and geographic communities may no longer be the places where we spend most of our time (although Covid-19 has certainly forced many people to experience and rethink the balance of work and life at home). Boyd and Angelique (2002, 2007), and Boyd (2011a, 2011b, 2014), have shown that organization studies and community psychology are complementary fields.

As I wrote in 2014,

> Community psychologists have much to share with individuals in fields related to the study of organizations and to the organizational literature at large. Community scholars have knowledge, skills, and abilities in a variety of content

> areas including empowerment, sense of community, stress and coping, diversity, ecological analysis, and prevention. Content expertise, methodological skill, and a humanistic worldview are things that community scholars can share with organization researchers. Similarly, organization scholars can share concepts, skills, and abilities with community psychologists that can be fruitful for the development of building community in organizations.

As scholars and researchers, we have an opportunity to investigate phenomena of importance, and building community at work is certainly worthy of our time and energy. As I consider the landscape of the current academic literature and scholarly discourse, I think there are several paths forward for our collective research pursuits.

Community Psychologists

In general, community psychologists should continue to investigate a variety of phenomena in organizational settings, and at the same time import and investigate organization studies, management, and public management concepts, models, and theories into community psychology scholarship and practice. In a similar vein, organizational scholars should look to community psychology for guidance on many of the most pressing human-centric issues that we face today. The boundary space between these fields continues to provide a fruitful and meaningful space for study and understanding.

Community psychologists should consider attending and contributing scholarship in a variety of venues where organization and management scholars showcase their work. The Academy of Management (AOM; Aom.org) Annual Meeting, regional Academy of Management Conferences (e.g., Eastern, Midwest, Western, Southwest), the International Association for Business and Society (iabs.net), the Public Management Research Conference (PMRC; pmranet.org), the International Research Society for Public Management (IRSPM; irspm.org), and the Association for Research on Nonprofit Organizations and Voluntary Action (ARNOVA; arnova.org) are great spaces to share your work and learn about the latest management science discoveries. Each of these associations has affiliations with, or sponsor, peer-reviewed publications, including some of the top journals within their disciplinary homes (e.g., *Academy of Management Review*, *Academy of Management Journal*, *Academy of Management Perspectives*, *Academy of Management Annals*, *Academy of Management Discoveries*, *Journal of Business and Society*, *Journal of Public Administration Research and Theory*, *Public Management Review*, *Nonprofit and Voluntary Sector Quarterly*). There are many other excellent organization studies, management, and public management journals, and most of them can be found on the Australian Business Deans Council List (abdc.edu.au/abdc-journal-quality-list), and by consulting other available sources on the Internet. The *Harvard Business Review* (hbr.org) and the *Economist* (economist.com) are excellent popular press publications that help you peer into the latest thinking in management, business, and economics topics.

Management and Business Scholars

Management, business, and organization studies scholars should consider attending and contributing scholarship in the places where community psychologists commiserate. The Biennial Society for Community Research and Action Conference (SCRA27.org), the American Psychological Association (APA.org), and regional U.S. psychological associations are excellent places to contribute your work. The Society for Community Action and Research sponsors the *American Journal of Community Psychology*, and the *Journal of Community Psychology*, the *Journal of Prevention and Intervention in the Community*, and the *Journal of Community and Applied Social Community Psychology* are other good venues to explore for publication. Additional community psychology journals, and related journals, are listed on the SCRA27.org website (https://scra27.org/publications/other-journals-relevant-community-psychology). The Society for Community Action and Research official newsletter, *The Community Psychologist* (https://www.scra27.org/publications/tcp), is an excellent resource for those who would like to keep abreast of current issues and topics in the field of community psychology.

I also think there are some immediate research gaps that are open for exploration on the topic of community at work. At this point in time, I feel that a strong case has been made that a psychological sense of community and a sense of community responsibility are constructs that can predict important individual outcomes in organizations (e.g., psychological well-being, thriving, job satisfaction, organizational citizenship behaviors, job engagement), and I believe that more individual cognitive, affective (emotional), and behavioral outcomes can be studied. However, besides recent work by me and Sharon Larson (Boyd and Larson, 2023a, 2023b), we know a lot less about the specific antecedent factors that lead to building community at work. These recent studies show that many antecedent factors appear to influence the building of community at work, and the antecedent variables discussed in this book (and in the recent studies) can serve as excellent specific areas of future investigation. For example, I think we need to know more about the initial development process of experiences of community. Livne-Tarandach and Jazaieri (2021) published a wonderful study (in the *Academy of Management Journal*—a top management publication), where they demonstrated that simple actions like eye contact, smiling, name recognition, and the use of small artifacts can serve as scaffolds that mobilize actors to create a web of connections, which then led to an organization-wide swift sense of community. This study gives us a sense of the kinds of actions that can spark an experience of community, but perhaps there are additional early development factors to be explored, and we have a lot to learn about what to do next in order to sustain experiences of community after initial inception to maintenance and growth over the long term within organizations. I also believe there is much to learn on the consequence side of the community experience model beyond individual outcomes. The model expresses that additional outcomes should be achieved as a function of experiencing community within the work unit, divisions and departments, the organization as a whole, and outcomes for stakeholders beyond the boundary of the organization. There are plenty of analogous guides from the community psychology literature in terms of neighborhood, town, and community outcomes, but empirical studies of organizational outcomes, within various units, or beyond the boundary of the organization are currently unknown. For example, within departments and divisions of organizations, how do experiences of community relate to employee performance and group performance within the unit, acceptance rates of new hires, absenteeism, turnover, and safety? For the organization, do community experiences predict earnings per share, sales growth, customer/client/citizen satisfaction, other critical financial metrics, and achievement of sustainability goals? Beyond the boundary of the organization, how do experiences of community at work impact interaction and effective relationships with specific external stakeholders to the organization, the culture and functioning of the local community, and the reputation of the organization to the general populace?

We also have much to learn in terms of how experiences of community relate to many concepts within the field of community psychology and organization, business, and management studies. For example, in community psychology, how do empowerment, gender, intersectionality, racial reckoning, sustainability, justice, neurodiversity, resilience, hope, and many other concepts, models, and theories relate to experiences of community in organizations? Many of these topics apply to organization and management scholars as well, but in addition, how do virtual work, entrepreneurship, employee benefits, extreme work conditions, disaster management, artificial intelligence, strategic planning, and leadership relate to experiences of community in organizations? And is there a "dark side" when attempting to build community at work?

Areas of Immediate Attention

Human Resource Management

There are also a few specific areas of inquiry that warrant immediate and sustained attention where community experience concepts have gained some academic traction. The first is in the field of human resource management. A recent collaborative study by psychologists and management scholars (Jonsen et al., 2022) showed that a sense of community and a sense of community responsibility may play an important role in the strategic human resource management "black box." The black box is characterized in the human resource management literature as a space of mediators between high-performance work systems and organizational outcomes. A high-performance work systems could be any "system" of an organization that is thought to produce high-performance work processes and outcomes, and it could theoretically be in any domain of the organization.

In HR, high-performance systems typically refer to state-of-the-art HR practices in recruiting, hiring, training, compensation, HR information systems, and so on, and the presence of these state-of-the-art "best practices" should lead to improved organizational outcomes. For example, a new state-of-the-art wellness program should lead to improved psychological and physical health of employees, which should then lead to improved organizational productivity and performance (among other important outcomes). Boxall and Macky (2009) argue that high-performance work systems contain ambiguous concepts and too often comprise an eclectic and contentious set of "best practices," and that researchers should focus on the social and psychological processes of workers when seeking to explain connections between human resource management systems and employee and operational outcomes. Therefore, HR scholars are calling for a greater understanding of psychological factors that predict organizational outcomes, regardless of the specific HR system that is in place.

In other words, scholars are saying that we need to pay more attention to the psychological processes than the HR systems per se, because psychological constructs are much more likely to have reliable and valid measures (compared with best practice HR systems that can vary significantly from one organization to another), and therefore relationships with organizational outcomes will likely be more valid as well. The recent study by Jonsen et al. (2022) showed that community experiences play a mediating role between the relationship of high-involvement workplaces (a concept that HR professionals are trying to create in organizations) and organizational outcomes. First, the study showed that experiences of community were related to high-involvement climate. More specifically, a sense of community and a sense of community responsibility were both related to high-involvement organizational climates that contain high levels of information, knowledge, and rewards for employees. Further, a sense of community responsibility was the only psychological construct that mediated the relationship between high-involvement climate and the outcome measures of organizational citizenship behaviors (above and beyond actions of employees that help the organization and its members). This study is important because it helps to set the stage for further investigations in the field of human resource management that assist us on a quest to understand the most important psychological variables in workplaces for the achievement of individual and organizational outcomes, and as we attempt to learn how HR best practices align to those psychological constructs.

Organizational Behavior

A second area that is especially fertile ground for further exploration is the field of organizational behavior (OB). As noted previously, several studies have already shown that community experiences are excellent predictors of individual well-being and behavioral outcomes compared with long-studied and highly regarded constructs in the field of management. This includes affective organizational commitment (AOC) and organizational identification (OI), which are perhaps two of the most studied and respected constructs in the disciplines of management and organizational behavior. However, in my opinion, we need more studies that continue to empirically test the comparative predictive capacity of community experience variables in relation to AOC and OI, and other mainstream organizational behavior constructs, on outcomes of importance (especially organization-level outcomes), and we need more studies that help us understand the theories that drive these constructs, and the organizational context features that help to stimulate their comparative presence in employees. At the intersection of HR and OB, I am in the midst of new work with Rick Jonsen and Tom Calvard that attempts to explain a pressing need for community experience measures in annual employee climate surveys. HR departments routinely conduct annual climate surveys to understand employee satisfaction, morale, and in short, the "pulse" of the employee culture. In our review of contemporary climate surveys, we noticed that they sometimes measure concepts like affective commitment and organizational identification (usually with single items compared with full academically validated scales), and that measures of belonging or membership are included. However, because community experience constructs are more recent in the academic literature, they have yet to make their way into mainstream employee climate surveys. And, given that experiences of community have demonstrated excellent predictive capacity of employee well-being and behavioral engagement, it makes sense that we should explore their use in organizational climate surveys. I feel like the budding research in this area has put us on the precipice of a potential groundbreaking finding in organizational behavior and management, and if more confirmation and understanding can be derived, experience-of-community constructs have an enormous potential upside in management scholarship and practice.

Public Management and Public Administration

A third area that is currently percolating and growing is the field of public management and public administration. A series of studies have already shown that experience-of-community measures robustly predict public and nonprofit employee well-being and behavioral outcomes compared with the concept of public service motivation (PSM), which, like AOC and OI in management, is perhaps the most studied motivational concept in public management. Like my earlier comments in relation to AOC and OI, more comparative studies are needed. However, perhaps even more important are the growing findings around a sense of community responsibility. The idea of "responsibility toward others" is especially pervasive in public management scholarship because of the fact that public and nonprofit institutions have direct missions that serve common-good goals associated with environmental, social, and economic justice. In fact, this is why the concept of public service motivation (the motivation to serve others by joining public service organizations) has gained so much attention in public management scholarship. Several recent studies have shown that a sense of community responsibility is a key driver of behavioral action for nonprofit and public leaders and employees. Thus, when employees and administrators experience a sense of community responsibility (which, remember, is facilitated by organizational context features that signal responsibility matters in this work setting), they are more apt to act toward the achievement of the goals of the organization. And, the achievement of public and nonprofit sector organizational goals means that citizens and clients are receiving the services and care that they need.

Also, the field of public administration more generally (which is an interdisciplinary field situated primarily between political science and public management) could benefit by increased studies that incorporate community experience factors. I recently published a paper with Eric Martin (2020) that focused on public sector responses to the Covid-19 pandemic, which made it clear that a sense of community responsibility is crucial for mitigating the effects of viral spread. We especially noted that in contexts of crisis, a critical action of public administrators is to clarify the referent of responsibility for the specific crisis, and then make sure that the appropriate level of governance acts toward the crisis. In the case of Covid-19, the crisis was at an international referent (across the whole world). However, international governance institutions did not have the authority to act on behalf of nation-states. Therefore, the appropriate crisis referent for the pandemic was comprised of the executive leaders of nations (in cooperation with each other and with international institutions). Yet, as we unfortunately experienced as citizens, we did not have an effective coordinated response between countries, and in many countries the executive leaders did not take appropriate action to ameliorate the pandemic. Instead, many citizens experienced a dispersed set of actions (e.g., in specific states in the United States, or by the private sector) that created confusion and a much less effective mitigation of the crisis.

Eric also recently coauthored a paper with Kateryna Zarembo (2023) that studied the crisis situation in Ukraine. They surveyed a variety of citizens in relation to their civic action during the crisis and found that Ukraine's massive civic engagement and collective action against Russian aggression were driven by a startling picture of grassroots activism. This finding was in contrast to traditional definitions of civil society that focus on citizen attachment and engagement in formal public and nonprofit institutions and showed that an understanding of civil society is complemented by a sense of community and community responsibility. In other words, their work is showing that civil society may not rest on its institutions per se but may be grounded (or also grounded) in psychological experiences of responsibility for collectives that citizens inhabit. Eric, Kateryna, and I are also starting a new study that directly tests propositions of the community experience model with data collected during the Ukrainian crisis, which has promise of showing that civil society may be generated from psychological states of community responsibility toward specific referents (i.e., the family, my neighborhood, my town/city, my region of Ukraine, the nation). Finally, I am also working with Jaclyn Piatak on a study that is investigating experiences of community in relation to prosocial actions in voluntary, political, and community engagement. This work is especially interesting because it studies citizen actions in relation to political worldviews and behaviors, which is a topic of political science and public administration that has not yet been studied.

Community Psychology

A fourth area is specifically the field of community psychology. As you have learned throughout this book, much of the research on the community experience model has occurred in organizational contexts since 2010. And, the literature on experiences of community is primarily dispersed across management, public management, community psychology, and a few other fields. And, while many studies of a psychological sense of community continue to be published in a wide variety of contexts in the field of community psychology, fewer studies are specifically studying a sense of community responsibility and the grounding theoretical arguments in the full community experience model. In the field of community psychology, I think we need more scholarship that studies both a sense of community and a sense of community responsibility (grounded in the community experience model), compared with studies that solely focus on a sense of community. And, I think we need more explorations of a sense of community responsibility in studies of the family, neighborhoods, towns, cities, and many other collective forms besides companies and public management settings. Community psychologists, like management and public management scholars, are interested in knowing how to improve individual well-being and behavioral action, given that a sense of community responsibility has shown impressive prediction of behavioral action in organizational settings when directly compared with a sense of community, I believe that we need to employ the construct of a sense of community responsibility in many more community psychology studies.

There are certainly many more domains of scholarship where we can apply the community experience model, but beyond scholarly endeavors, I think it is important for us to consider integrating the logics of community at work in our higher education degree programs. If you are a community psychology professor in an academic setting (or in an arts and sciences department), I hope you might consider incorporating more readings, case studies, and community-based learning experiences in private sector organizations (in addition to nonprofit, government, grassroots, and other community organizational forms). We need more community psychologists (and humanists, social scientists, and others) to consider private sector and corporate careers (including management consulting) as a way to help transform the narratives and actions of business and management. If you are a student in community psychology, psychology, or arts and sciences, I urge you to ask for readings, assignments, and experiences that help you to learn more about the application of your discipline in businesses and corporations (and other organizational forms). If you are a professor or student in a management or business program, I urge you to learn more about the field of community psychology (and of course the community experience model), and intentionally integrate social science literature and ideas into your courses and experiences. I also encourage you to create a stronger integration of nonprofit, government, and community organizations into your program experiences so students are exposed to a wide variety of organizational forms. If you are a member of the Association to Advance Collegiate Schools of Business (AACSB), you can do this under the premise of integrating sustainable development goals into your programs, and increasing social impact, which, as you know, is a new standard for AACSB accreditation. However, while levers like accreditation are fine (I guess), I think a consideration of integrating experiences of community at work, and community psychology ideas in general, is a matter of "what's good for your students." Finally, if you are a practitioner (an employee, manager, leaders, consultant, etc.), I urge you to continue to educate yourself from various lenses and vantage points. It is easy to rely on things we learned in the past, or the best practices within our disciplines, but a lot of intellectual fruit exists beyond the boundaries of our fields. I hope this book has helped you to see that in relation to experiences of community in organizations, and I urge you to continue to engage in a quest for knowledge, no matter where it derives from, as an enlightened way to navigate your life journey.

As I mentioned in the introduction to this book, I once took a first step forward to investigate the intersection of community psychology and organization studies, and shortly after, a deep dive into the psychological experiences of community at work. It is hard to believe that almost 20 years has passed since I took that first step, and I wouldn't trade it for anything. Understanding experiences of community, and helping you understand how to build them in organizations, has been one of the best activities of my life, and I hope this book has stimulated new ways of thinking about how to conceive and build better human-centric cultures at work. I can't think of anything more important, beyond mere survival, than helping those around us to live fulfilling and thriving lives. And, I certainly believe that creating communities at work is one of the ways in which we can do that. I hope that after reading this book you feel even more inspired to do that too!

References

Adams, C. A., Muir, S., & Hoque, Z. (2014). Measurement of sustainability performance in the public sector. *Sustainability Accounting, Management and Policy Journal*, *5*(1), 46–67.

Adelman, C. (1993) Kurt Lewin and the Origins of Action Research. *Educational Action Research*, *1*, 7–24. doi:10.1080/0965079930010102

Adler, P., & Kwon, S., (2002). Social capital: Prospects for a new concept. *Academy of Management Review*, 27(1), 17–40.

Albanesi, C., Cicognani, E., & Zani, B. (2007). Civic involvement, sense of community and social well-being in adolescence. *Journal of Community & Applied Social Psychology*, *17*, 387–406.

Allen, N. J., & Meyer, J. P. (1990). The measurement and antecedents of affective, continuance and normative commitment to the organization. *Journal of Occupational Psychology*, *63*, 1–18.

Anderson, C., & Brion, S. (2014). Perspectives on power in organizations. *Annual Review of Organizational Psychology and Organizational Behavior*, *1*(1), 67–97.

Angelique, H., & Kyle, K. (2002). Monterey declaration of critical community psychology. *The Community Psychologist* [A publication of the Society for Community Research and Action, Division 27 of the American Psychological Association], *35*(1), 35–36.

Argyris, C. (1957). *Personality and organization: The conflict between system and the individual.* New York: Harper & Row.

Ashforth, B. E., & Mael, F. (1989). Social identity theory and the organization. *Academy of Management Review*, *14*, 20–39.

Atkinson, C. (2007). Trust and the psychological contract. *Employee Relations*, *29*, 227–246.

Bal, P., De Lange, A., Jansen, P. G., & Van Der Velde, M. (2008). Psychological contract breach and job attitudes: A meta-analysis of age as a moderator. *Journal of Vocational Behavior*, *72*, 143–158.

Bandura, A. (2001). Social cognitive theory: An agentic perspective. *Annual Review of Psychology*, *52*(1), 1–26.

Banyard, V. L., & Miller, K. E. (1998). The powerful potential of qualitative research for community psychology. *American Journal of Community Psychology, 26*(4), 485–505.

Barnard, C. I. (1968). *The functions of the executive*. Cambridge, MA: Harvard University Press.

Beal, D., Cohen, R., Burke, M., & McLendon, C. (2003). Cohesion and performance in groups: A meta-analytic clarification of construct relations. *Journal of Applied Psychology, 88*(6), 989–1004.

Beals, A. M., Thomas, D., Fernández, J. S., Wilson, C. L., & Palmer, G. (2021). Resisting the coloniality and colonialism of a westernized community psychology: Toward a critical racial justice praxis. *Global Journal of Community Psychology Practice, 12*(2), 1–22.

Bellah, R. N., Madsen, R., Sullivan, W. M., Swidler, A., & Tipton, S. M. (1985). *Habits of the heart: Individualism and commitment in American life*. Berkeley: University of California.

Bertram, C. (2004). *Routledge philosophy guidebook to Rousseau and the social contract*. London: Routledge.

Bess, K. D., Prilleltensky, I., Perkins, D. D., & Collins, L. V. (2009). Participatory organizational change in community-based health and human services: From tokenism to political engagement. *American Journal of Community Psychology, 43*(1/2), 134–148.

Block, P. (2008). *Community: The structure of belonging*. San Francisco: Berrett-Koehler.

Bond, M. A., & Harrell, S. P. (2006). Diversity challenges in community research and action: The story of a special issue of *AJCP*. *American Journal of Community Psychology*, 37, 157–166.

Bond, M. A., & Haynes-Baratz, M. C. (2022). Mobilizing bystanders to address microaggressions in the workplace: The case for a systems-change approach to Getting A (Collective) GRIP. *American Journal of Community Psychology*, 69, 221–238.

Boxall, P., & Macky, K. (2009). Research and theory on high-performance work systems: Progressing the high-involvement stream. *Human Resource Management Journal, 19*, 3–23.

Boyd, N. (2009, August 7–11). *Seeing organizations as communities: Community perspectives on public/nonprofit management*. Panelist for a session sponsored by the Public and Non-Profit division of the Academy of Management. Academy of Management Conference. Chicago, IL, United States.

Boyd, N. (2011a). Organization development in community contexts. *Journal of Prevention and Intervention in the Community, 39*(1), 1–4.

Boyd, N. (2011b). Helping organizations help others: Organization development as a facilitator of social change. *Journal of Prevention and Intervention in the Community, 39*(1), 5–18.

Boyd, N. (2014). A ten-year retrospective of organization studies in community psychology: Content, theory, and impact. *Journal of Community Psychology, 42*(2), 237–254.

Boyd, N., & Angelique, H. (2002). Rekindling the discourse: Organization studies in community psychology. *Journal of Community Psychology*, *30*(4), 325–348.

Boyd, N., & Angelique, H. (2007). Resuming the dialogue on organization studies and community psychology: An introduction to the special issue. *Journal of Community Psychology*, *35*(3), 281–285.

Boyd, N., Bess, K., Evans, S., Bond, M., & Griffith, D. (2007, June 6–10). Forward we march: Organization studies and community psychology. Panel at the 21st Society for Community Action and Research Biennial Conference. Pasadena, CA, United States.

Boyd, N., & Bright, D. (2007). Appreciative inquiry as a mode of action research in community psychology. *Journal of Community Psychology*, *35*(8), 1019–1036.

Boyd, N., & Gessner, B. (2013). Human resource performance metrics: Methods & processes that demonstrate you care. *Cross Cultural Management: An International Journal*, *20*(2), 251–273.

Boyd, N., & Larson, S. (2023a). Building community at work: An exploratory study in healthcare system management. *Journal of Community Psychology*, *51*(5), 2276–2299.

Boyd, N., & Larson, S. (2023b). Organizational cultures that support community: Does the competing values framework help us understand experiences of community at work? *Journal of Community Psychology*, *51*(4), 1695–1715.

Boyd, N., & Nowell, B. (2011, June 16–19). *Exploring sense of community as resource versus responsibility in organizations and collaborative settings*. Society for Community Research and Action Conference. Chicago, IL, United States.

Boyd, N., & Nowell, B. (2014). Psychological sense of community: A new construct for the field of management. *Journal of Management Inquiry*, *23*(2), 107–122.

Boyd, N., & Nowell, B. (2017). Testing a theory of sense of community and community responsibility in organizations: An empirical assessment of predictive capacity on employee well-being and organizational citizenship. *Journal of Community Psychology*, *45*(2), 210–229.

Boyd, N. M., & Martin, E. C. (2020). Sense of community responsibility at the forefront of crisis management. *Administrative Theory & Praxis*, *44*(1), 71–83. doi:10.1080/10841806.2020.1765288

Boyd, N., & Nowell, B. (2020). Public service motivation, sense of community, sense of community responsibility, organizational commitment, and identification: Testing an integrated model of employee well-being and engagement in a public service work context. *Public Management Review*, *22*(7–8), 1024–1050.

Boyd, N., Nowell, B., Bess, K., & Lardon, C. (2008, August 8–13). Bringing community action and research to the Academy of Management. A symposium session sponsored by the Public and Non-Profit division of the Academy of Management. Proceedings of the 60th Academy of Management Conference. Anaheim, CA, United States.

Boyd, N., Nowell, B., Bess, K., Evans, S., & Lardon, C. (2009, August 11). *Seeing organizations as communities: Community perspectives on public/nonprofit management.* Panel sponsored by the Public and Non-Profit division of the Academy of Management. Proceedings of the 61st Academy of Management Conference. Chicago, IL, United States.

Boyd, N., Nowell, B., Yang, Z., & Hano, M. (2018). Sense of community, sense of community responsibility, and public service motivation as predictors of employee well-being and engagement in public sector organizations. *American Review of Public Administration*, *48*(5), 428–443.

Brincker, B., & Pedersen, L. H. (2020). Attraction and attrition under extreme conditions: Integrating insights on PSM, SOC-R, SOC and excitement motivation. *Public Management Review*, *22*(7), 1051–1069. doi:10.1080/14719037.2020.1740306

Bright, D. S., Cooperrider, D. L., & Galloway, W. B. (2006). Appreciative inquiry in the Office of Research and Development: Improving the collaborative capacity of organization. *Public Performance and Management Review*, *29*, 285–306.

Brodsky, A. E., O'Campo, J., & Aronson, R. E. (1999). PSOC in community context: Multi-level correlates of a measure of psychological sense of community in low-income, urban neighborhoods. *Journal of Community Psychology*, *27*, 659–680.

Burke, W. W. (2002). *Organization change: Theory and practice*. Thousand Oaks, CA: Sage.

Burr, V. (2015). *Social constructionism*. London: Routledge.

Burroughs, S. M., & Eby, L. T. (1998). Psychological sense of community at work: A measurement system and explanatory framework. *Journal of Community Psychology*, *26*(6), 509–532.

Burton, M., Boyle, S., Harris, C., & Kagan, C. (2007). Community psychology in Britain. In S. Reich, M. Riemer, I. Prilleltensky, & M. Montero (Eds.), *International community psychology* (pp. 219–237). New York: Kluwer/Springer.

Cadbury, D. (2010). *Chocolate wars: The 150-year rivalry between the world's greatest chocolate makers*. New York: Public Affairs.

Cantano, V., Pretty, G., Southwell, R., & Cole, G. (1993). Sense of community and union participation. *Psychological Reports*, *72*, 333–334.

Cameron, K. S., & Quinn, R. E. (1999). *Diagnosing and changing organizational culture*. Addison-Wesley.

Carron, A. V. (1982). Cohesiveness in sport groups: Interpretations and considerations. *Journal of Sport Psychology*, *4*, 123–138.

Carver, C. S. (1998). Resilience and thriving: Issues, models, and linkages. *Journal of Social Issues*, *54*, 245–266.

Chalofsky, N. (2010). *Meaningful workplaces: Reframing how and where we work*. San Francisco: Jossey-Bass.

Chavis, D. M., Lee, K. S., & Acosta J. D. (2008). *The sense of community (SCI) revised: The reliability and validity of the SCI-2*. Paper presented at the 2nd International Community Psychology Conference. Lisboa, Portugal.

Chavis, D., & Wandersman, A. (1990). Sense of community in the urban environment: A catalyst for participation and community development. *American Journal of Community Psychology, 18*, 15–81.

Chipuer, H. M., & Pretty, G. M. H. (1999). A review of the Sense of Community Index: Current uses, factor structure, reliability, and further development. *Journal of Community Psychology, 27*, 643–658.

Chouinard, Y. (2016). *Let my people go surfing: The education of a reluctant businessman—including 10 more years of business unusual.* New York: Penguin Publishing Group.

Christens, B. D. (2019). *Community power and empowerment.* New York: Oxford University Press.

Ciofalo, N., Dudgeon, P., & Nikora, L. W. (2022). Indigenous community psychologies, decolonization, and radical imagination within ecologies of knowledges. *American Journal of Community Psychology, 69*, 283–293.

Cohen, A. (2007). Commitment before and after: An evaluation and reconceptualization of organizational commitment. *Human Resource Management Review, 17*, 336–354.

Coleman, J. S. (1988). Social capital in the creation of human capital. *American Journal of Sociology, 94*, 95–120.

Collins, C. R., Macbeth, J., Morgan, A. R., Kohl, R., & Kenney, T. M. (2023). Disrupting White racial dominance: How White antiracists challenge the racial status quo in interpersonal relationships. *Journal of Community Psychology, 51*, 103–119.

Cooperrider, D. L. (1990). Positive image, positive action: The affirmative basis of organizing. In S. Srivastva & D. L. Cooperrider (Eds.), *Appreciative management and leadership: The power of positive thought and action in organizations* (pp. 91–125). San Francisco: Jossey-Bass.

Cooperrider, D. L., & Avital, M. (Eds.). (2004). Constructive discourse and human organization. Boston: Elsevier Ltd.

Cooperrider, D. L., Whitney, D., & Stavros, J. M. (2003). *Appreciative inquiry handbook: The first in a series of AI workbooks for leaders of change.* Bedford Heights, OH: Lakeshore Communications.

Costa, P. L., McDuffie, J. W., Brown, S. E. V., He, Y., Ikner, B. N., Sabat, I. E., & Miner, K. N. (2023). Microaggressions: Mega problems or micro issues? A meta-analysis. *Journal of Community Psychology, 51*, 137–153.

Csikszentmihalyi, M. (1990). *Flow: The psychology of optimal experience.* New York: Harper Collins.

Cummings, T., & Worley, C. (2015). Organization development and change. Stamford, CT: Cengage Learning.

Dalton, E., Elias, M. J., Wandersman, A. (2007). *Community psychology: Linking individuals and communities.* Stamford, CT: Wadsworth.

DeNisi, A. S., & Murphy, K. R. (2017). Performance appraisal and performance management: 100 years of progress? *Journal of Applied Psychology, 102*(3), 421–433.

Diener, E., Suh, E. M., Lucas, R. E., & Smith, H. L. (1999). Subjective well-being: Three decades of progress. *Psychological Bulletin, 125*, 276–302.

Doolittle, R., & MacDonald, D. (1978). Communication and a sense of community in a metropolitan neighborhood: A factor analytic examination. *Communication Quarterly*, *26*, 2–7.

Drucker, P. F. (1946). *Concept of the corporation*. New York: John Day Company.

Ellaway, A., Macintyre, S., & Kearns, A. (2001). Perceptions of place and health in socially contrasting neighborhoods. *Urban Studies*, *38*(12), 2219–2316.

Festinger L. (1950). Informal social communication. *Psychological Review*, *57*, 271–282.

Festinger, L. (1957). *A theory of cognitive dissonance*. Stanford, CA: Stanford University Press.

Fisher, A. T., Sonn, C. C., & Bishop, B. J. (Eds.). (2002). *Psychological sense of community: Research, applications, and implications*. New York: Plenum.

Fisher, A. T., Sonn, C. C., & Evans, S. D. (2007). The place and function of power in community psychology: Philosophical and practical issues. *Journal of Community and Applied Social Psychology*, *17*, 258–267.

Follett, M. P. (1918). *The new state: Group organization the solution of popular government*. New York: Longmans, Green and Co.

French, W. L., & Bell, C. H. (1994). *Organization development: Behavioral science interventions for organization improvement* (5th ed.). Englewood Cliffs, NJ: Prentice Hall.

Friedman, M. (1970, September 13). A Friedman doctrine: The social responsibility of business is to increase its profits. *The New York Times Magazine*. https://www.nytimes.com/1970/09/13/archives/a-friedman-doctrine-the-social-responsibility-of-business-is-to.html.

Fujimoto, Y., Azmat, F., & Subramaniam, N. (2019). Creating community-inclusive organizations: Managerial accountability framework. *Business & Society*, *58*, 683–882.

Garrett, L. E., Spreitzer, G. M., & Bacevice, P. A. (2017). Co-constructing a sense of community at work: The emergence of community in coworking spaces. *Organization Studies*, *38*(6), 821–842.

Glynn, T. (1981). Psychological sense of community: Measurement and application. *Human Relations*, *34*, 780–818.

Gummesson, E. (2000). *Qualitative methods in management research* (2nd ed.). London: SAGE Publications.

Hamel, G. (2009). Moon shots for management. *Harvard Business Review*, *87*(2), 91–98.

Harré, N., Blythe, C., McLean, L., & Khan, S. (2022). A people-focused systems approach to sustainability. *American Journal of Community Psychology*, *69*, 114–133.

Harrison, J. S., & Freeman, R. E. (2004). Is organizational democracy worth the effort? *Academy of Management Executive*, *18*, 49–53.

Hart, E., & Bond, M. (1995). *Action research for health and social care: A guide to practice*. London: Open University Press.

Heckscher, C. (2015). *Trust in a complex world: Enriching community*. New York: Oxford.

Hendry, J., Hiller, T., Martin, E., & Boyd, N. (2017). Context and pedagogy: A quarter century of change in an undergraduate introductory management course. *Journal of Management Education*, *41*(3), 346–384.

Ho, V. T. (2005). Social influence on evaluations of psychological contract fulfillment. *Academy of Management Review*, *30*, 113–128.

Hughey, J., Speer, P. W., & Peterson, N. A. (1999). Sense of community in community organizations: Structure and evidence of validity. *Journal of Community Psychology*, 27(1), 97–113.

Jason, L. A., Stevens, E., & Ram, D. (2015). Development of a three-factor psychological sense of community scale. *Journal of Community Psychology*, *43*, 973–985.

Jonsen, R., Boyd, N., Oikelome, F., & Trimble, D. (2022). Exploring the strategic human resource management black box by investigating the role of community experiences in high involvement work practices. *Journal of Community Psychology*. doi:10.1002/jcop.22965

Kallas, J., Ritchie, K., & Friedman, E. (2022). *Labor action tracker: Annual report 2022*. Ithaca, NY: ILR Worker Institute, Cornell University ILR School.

Kelly, J. (2019). More than half of U.S. workers are unhappy in their jobs: Here's why and what needs to be done now. *Forbes*. Accessed Oct 25, 2019. https://www.forbes.com/sites/jackkelly/2019/10/25/more-than-half-of-us-workers-are-unhappy-in-their-jobs-heres-why-and-what-needs-to-be-done-now/.

Kelly, J. G., Azelton, L. S., Lardon, C., Mock, L. O., Tandon, S. D., & Thomas, M. (2004). On community leadership: Stories about collaboration in action research. *American Journal of Community Psychology*, *33*(3–4), 205–216.

Keyes, C. L. M., & Haidt, J. (2003). *Flourishing: Positive psychology and the life well-lived*. Washington, DC: American Psychological Association.

Keys, C. B., & Frank, S. (1987). Community psychology and the study of organizations: A reciprocal relationship. *American Journal of Community Psychology*, *15*, 239–251.

Klein, H. J., Molloy, J. C., & Brinsfield, C. T. (2012). Reconceptualizing workplace commitment to redress a stretched construct: Revisiting assumptions and removing confounds. *Academy of Management Review*, *37*, 130–151.

Klein, K. J., & D'Aunno, T. A. (1986). Psychological sense of community in the workplace. *Journal of Community Psychology*, *14*(4), 365–377.

Kloos, B., Hill, J., Thomas, E., Wandersman, A., Elias, M. J., & Dalton, J. H. (2012). *Community psychology*. Belmont, CA: Cengage Learning.

Kresse, K. (2007). *Philosophising in Mombasa: Knowledge, Islam, and Intellectual Practice on the Swahili Coast*. Edinburgh: Edinburgh University Press

Landrum, R. E., Brakke, K., & McCarthy, M. A. (2019). The pedagogical power of storytelling. *Scholarship of Teaching and Learning in Psychology*, *5*(3), 247–253.

Lewin, K. (1946). Action research and minority problems. *Journal Social Issues*, *4*, (2) 34–46.

Lewin, K. (1947). Frontiers in group dynamics: Concept, method, and reality in social science; equilibrium and social change. *Human Relations*, *1*(1), 5–41.

Lewin, K. (1951). Field Theory in Social Science. New York: Harper.

Livne-Tarandach, R., & Jazaieri, H. (2021). Swift sense of community: Resourcing artifacts for rapid community emergence in a temporary organization. *Academy of Management Journal, 64*, 1127–1163.

Long, D. A., & Perkins, D. D. (2003). Confirmatory factor analysis of the Sense of Community Index and development of a Brief SCI. *Journal of Community Psychology, 31*, 279–296.

Ludema, J. D., Whitney, D., Mohr, B. J., & Griffin, T. J. (2003). The Appreciative Inquiry Summit: A practitioner's guide for leading large-group change. San Francisco: Berrett-Koehler.

Lykes, M. B. (2017). Community-based and participatory action research: Community psychology collaborations within and across borders. In M. A. Bond, I. Serrano-García, C. B. Keys, & M. Shinn (Eds.), *APA handbook of community psychology: Methods for community research and action for diverse groups and issues* (pp. 43–58). Washington D.C.: APA.

Mahan, B. (2000). *An exploratory study of sense of community and trust in the university workplace*. Dissertation Abstracts International: Section B: The Sciences & Engineering, 41–61, 2256.

Mannarini, T. (2012). Power and participation in community research: Community profiling in Italy. In Lisa Goodson and Jenny Phillimore (Eds.), *Community research for participation* (pp. 139–154). Bristol: Policy Press.

Martin, E., & Zarembo, K. (2023). Civil society and sense of community in Ukraine: From dormancy to action. *European Societies*. doi:10.1080/14616696.2023.2185652

Maslow, A. H. (1943). A theory of human motivation. *Psychological Review, 50*(4), 370–396.

Maslow, A. H. (1965). *Eupsychian management: A journal*. Homewood, IL: Irwin.

Maslow, A. H. (1987). Motivation and personality (3rd ed.). Delhi, India: Pearson Education.

Maslow, A. H. (1998). *Maslow on management*. New York: John Wiley & Sons, Inc.

Masten, A. S., & Reed, M. J. (2002). Resilience in development. In C. R. Snyder & S. J. Lopez (Eds.), *Handbook of Positive Psychology*, 74–88. Oxford University Press, New York.

McClelland, D. C. (1961). *The achieving society*. Princeton, NJ: Van Nostrand.

McMillan, D. W., & Chavis, D. M. (1986). Sense of community: A definition and theory. *Journal of Community Psychology, 14*, 6–23.

Meinel, C., & Leifer, L. J. (2011). Design thinking research. In H. Plattner, C. Meinel, & L. J. Leifer (Eds.), *Design thinking: Understand, improve, apply* (pp. xiii–xxi). Berlin; Heidelberg: Springer-Verlag.

Miers, R., & Fisher, A. (2002). Being church and community: Psychological sense of community in a local parish. In A. Fisher & C. Sonn (Eds.), *Psychological sense of community: Research applications and implications* (pp. 123–140). New York: Plenum Publishers.

Miller, J. A. (1991). Experiencing management: A comprehensive, "hands-on" model for the introductory undergraduate management course. *Journal of Management Education*, *15*, 151–169.

Mintzberg, H. (2009, July–August). Rebuilding companies as communities. *Harvard Business Review*, 1–7.

Mittelbach, G. G., & McGill, B. J. (2019). *Community ecology*. Oxford: Oxford University Press.

Moran, T. E., Chen, C. Y. C., & Tryon, G. S (2018). Bully victimization, depression, and the role of protective factors among college LGBTQ students. *Journal of Community Psychology*, *46*, 871–884.

Morgan, G. (1986). Images of organization. Beverly Hills, CA: Sage

Moritsugu J., Vera E., Wong F., & Duffy K. G. (2014). *Community psychology*. Toronto, Ontario, Canada: Pearson.

Mowday, R. T., Steers, R. M., & Porter, L. W. (1979). The measurement of organizational commitment. *Journal of Vocational Behavior*, *14*, 224–247.

Neal, Z. P., & Neal, J. W. (2013). The (in)compatibility of diversity and sense of community. *American Journal of Community Psychology*. doi:10.1007/s10464-013-9608-0

Nelson, G., & Evans, S. D. (2014). Critical community psychology and qualitative research: A conversation. *Qualitative Inquiry*, *20*(2), 158–166.

Nelson, G., & Prilleltensky, I. (Eds.). (2010). *Community psychology: In pursuit of liberation and well-being* (2nd ed). Basingstoke, UK: Palgrave/Macmillan.

Nobles, W. W., Baloyi, L., & Sodi, T. (2016). Pan African humanness and Sakhu Djaer as praxis for indigenous knowledge systems. *Alternation Journal*, *18*, 36–59.

Nowell, B. (2009). Profiling capacity for coordination and systems change: The relative contribution of stakeholder relationships in interorganizational collaboratives. *American Journal of Community Psychology*, *44*(3/4), 196–212.

Nowell, B., & Boyd, N. (2010). Viewing community as responsibility as well as resource: Deconstructing the theoretical roots of psychological sense of community. *Journal of Community Psychology*, *38*(7), 828–841.

Nowell, B., & Boyd, N. (2014). Sense of community responsibility in community collaboratives: Advancing a theory of community as resource and responsibility. *American Journal of Community Psychology*, *54*, 229–242.

Nowell, B., Boyd, N., Hano, M., Izod, A., & Yang, Z. (2012, October 13–14). *Sense of community responsibility in collaborative partnerships: Preliminary findings*. Symposium presented at the Southeastern Ecological and Community Psychology Conference. Durham, NC, United States.

Nowell, B., Izod, A., Ngaruiya, K., & Boyd, N. (2016). Public service motivation and sense of community responsibility: Comparing two motivational constructs in understanding voluntary leadership within community collaboratives. *Journal of Public Administration Research and Theory*, *26*(4), 663–676

Obst, P., Smith, S. G., & Zinkiewicz, L. (2002). An exploration of sense of community, part 3: Dimensions and predictors of psychological sense of community in geographical communities. *Journal of Community Psychology*, *30*, 119–133.

Obst, P. L., & White, K. M. (2004). Revisiting the sense of community index: A confirmatory factor analysis. *Journal of Community Psychology*, *32*, 691–705.

Ogude, J., & Dyer, U. (2019). UTU/UBUNTU and community restoration: Narratives of survivors in Kenya's 2007 postelection violence. In J. Ogude (Ed.), *Ubuntu and the reconstitution of community* (pp. 206–226). Bloomington: Indiana University Press.

Oh, H., Labianca, G., & Chung, M. (2006). A multilevel model of group social capital. *Academy of Management Review*, *31*(3), 569–582.

Pedersen, L. H., Andersen, L. B., & Thomsen, N. (2020). Motivated to act and take responsibility—integrating insights from community psychology in PSM research. *Public Management Review*, *22*(7), 999–1023. doi:10.1080/14719037.2020.1740307

Patchen, M. (1970). *Participation, achievement, and involvement on the job*. Englewood Cliffs, NJ: Prentice Hall.

Perkins, D. D., Bess, K. D., Cooper, D. G., Jones, D. L., Armstead, T., & Speer, P. W. (2007). Community organizational learning: Case studies illustrating a three-dimensional model of levels and orders of change. *Journal of Community Psychology*, *35*(3), 303–238.

Perkins, D. D., Florin, P., Rich, R. C., Wandersman, A., & Chavis, D. (1990). Participation and the social and physical environment of residential blocks: Crime and community context. *American Journal of Community Psychology*, *18*, 83–115.

Peterson, N. A., Speer, P. W., & McMillan, D. W. (2008). Validation of a brief sense of community scale: Confirmation of the principal theory of sense of community. *Journal of Community Psychology*, *36*(1), 61–73.

Pfeffer, J. (2018). *Dying for a paycheck: How modern management harms employee health and company performance—and what we can do about it*. New York: Harper-Collins.

Porter, Michael E. (1985). *Competitive advantage: Creating and sustaining superior performance*. New York: Simon and Schuster.

Portney, K. E. (2013). Taking sustainable cities seriously: Economic development, the environment, and quality of life in American cities. Cambridge, MA: The MIT Press.

Pretty, G. M. (1990). Relating psychological sense of community to social climate characteristics. *Journal of Community Psychology*, *18*, 60–65.

Pretty, G., Andrews, L., & Collett, C. (1994). Exploring adolescents' sense of community and its relationship to loneliness. *Journal of Community Psychology*, *22*(4), 346–358.

Pretty, G., & McCarthy, M. (1991). Exploring psychological sense of community among men and women of the corporation. *Journal of Community Psychology*, *19*, 351–361.

Pretty, G., McCarthy, M., & Catano, V. (1992). Exploring environments and burnout: Gender considerations in the corporation. *Journal of Organizational Behavior*, *13*, 701–711.

Pretty, G. H., Conroy, C., Dugay, J., Fowler, K., & Williams, D. (1996). Sense of community and its relevance to adolescents of all ages. *Journal of Community Psychology*, *24*, 365–380.

Prezza, M., Amici, M., Roberti, T., & Tedeschi, C. (2001). Sense of community referred to the whole town: Its relations with neighboring, loneliness, life satisfaction and area of residence. *Journal of Community Psychology*, *29*, 29–52.

Prieto, L. C., & Phipps, S. T. A. (2016). Re-discovering Charles Clinton Spaulding's "The Administration of Big Business": Insight into early 20th century African American management thought. *Journal of Management History*, *22*(1), 73–90. doi:10.1108/JMH-01-2015-0004

Prieto, L. C., & Phipps, S. T. A. (2019). *African American management history: Insights on gaining a cooperative advantage*. Bingley, UK: Emerald Publishing.

Prilleltensky, I. (2012). Wellness as fairness. *American Journal of Community Psychology*, *49*, 1–21.

Prilleltensky, I. (2014). Meaning-making, mattering, and thriving in community psychology: From co-optation to amelioration and transformation. *Psychosocial Intervention*, *23*(2), 151–154. doi:10.1016/j.psi.2014.07.008

Prilleltensky, I. (2019). Mattering at the intersection of psychology, philosophy, and politics. *American Journal of Community Psychology*, 1–19.

Prilleltensky, I., & Prilleltensky, O. (2021). *How people matter: Why it affects health, happiness, love, work, and society*. Cambridge: Cambridge University Press.

Rigby, D. K., Sutherland, J., & Takeuchi, H. Embracing Agile: How to Master the Process That's Transforming Management. *Harvard Business Review*, *94*, no. 5:40–50.

Riger, S., & Lavrakas, P. (1981). Community ties: Patterns of attachment and social interaction in urban neighborhoods. *American Journal of Community Psychology*, *9*, 55–66.

Riketta, M. (2005). Organizational identification: A meta-analysis. *Journal of Vocational Behavior*, *66*, 358–384.

Robinson, S. L., & Morrison, E. W. (1995). Psychological contracts and OCB: The effects of unfulfilled obligations on civic virtue behavior. *Journal of Organizational Behavior*, *16*, 289–298.

Rousseau, D. M. (1995). *Psychological contracts in organizations*. London: SAGE.

Royal, M. A., & Rossi, R. J. (1996). Individual-level correlates of sense of community: Findings from workplace and school. *Journal of Community Psychology*, *24*(4), 395–416.

Sandler, J. (2007). Community-based practices: Integrating dissemination theory with critical theories of power and justice. *American Journal of Community Psychology*, *40*(3–4), 272–289.

Sarason, S. B. (1974). *The psychological sense of community: Prospects for a community psychology*. San Francisco: Jossey-Bass.

Sarason, S. B. (1976). Community psychology and the anarchist insight. *American Journal of Community Psychology*, *4*(3), 221–312

Schein, E. H. (1988). Process consultation. Reading, MA: Addison-Wesley.

Schein, E. H. (1992). *Organizational culture and leadership* (2nd ed.). Hoboken: Jossey-Bass.

Schuck, A. M. (2020). Examining the community consequences of arrests for low-level criminal activity. *Journal of Community Psychology*, *48*, 86–103.

Schutz, W. (1958). FIRO*: A three-dimensional theory of interpersonal behavior* (3rd ed). New York: Holt, Rinehart, and Winston.

Scott, V., & Wolfe, S. (2015). *Community psychology: Foundations for practice*. Thousand Oaks, CA: Sage.

Seligman, M. E. P. (2011). *Flourish*. New York: Free Press.

Seligman, M. E. P., & Csikszentmihalyi, M. (2000). Positive psychology: An introduction. *The American Psychologist*, *55*, 5–14

Sonn, C. (2002). Immigrant adaptation: Understanding the process through sense of community. In A. Fisher, C. Sonn, & B. Bishop's (Eds)., *Psychological sense of community: Research, applications, and implications* (pp. 205–222). New York: Plenum.

Sonn, C. C., & Fisher, A. T. (1996). Psychological sense of community in a politically constructed group. *Journal of Community Psychology*, *24*, 417–430.

Spreitzer, G. M., Sutcliffe, K., Dutton, J., Sonenshein, S., & Grant, A. M. (2005). A socially embedded model of thriving at work. *Organization Science*, *16*(5), 537–549.

Stewart, E. (2000). Thinking through others. In J. Rappaport & E. Seidman (Eds.), *Handbook of community psychology* (pp. 725–736). Boston: Springer.

Stivala, A., Robins, G., Kashima, Y., & Kirley, M. (2016). Diversity and community can coexist. *American Journal of Community Psychology*, *57*, 243–254.

Sutcliffe, K. M., & Vogus, T. J. (2003). Organizing for resilience. In K. S. Cameron, J. E. Dutton, & R. E. Quinn (Eds.), *Positive organizational scholarship: Foundations of a new discipline* (pp. 94–121). San Francisco: Berrett-Koehler.

Sutton, G., & Griffen, M. (2004). Integrating expectations, experiences and psychological contract violations. A longitudinal study of new professionals. *Journal of Occupational and Organizational Psychology*, 77, 493–514.

Treitler, P. C., Andrew Peterson, N., Howell, T. H., & Powell, K. G. (2018). Measuring sense of community responsibility in community-based prevention coalitions: An item response theory analysis. *American Journal of Community Psychology*, *62*(1–2), 110–120.

Trickett, E. J. (1996). A future for community psychology: The contexts of diversity and the diversity of contexts. *American Journal of Community Psychology*, *24*, 209–234.

Trickett, E. J. (2009). Community psychology: Individuals and interventions in community context. *Annual Review of Psychology*, *60*, 395–419.

Tschirhart, M., Boyd, N., Nowell, B., Bies, A., & Gronbjerg, K. (2010, August 6–10). *Community in theory/theory in community*. Panel discussant at the Academy of Management Annual Meeting. Montreal, Canada.

Turnley, W. H., & Feldman, D. C. (1999). The impact of psychological contract violations on exit, voice, loyalty, and neglect. *Human Relations*, *52*, 895–922.

Turnley, W. H., & Feldman, D. C. (2000). Re-examining the effects of psychological contract violations: Unmet expectations and job dissatisfaction as mediators. *Journal of Organizational Behavior*, *21*, 25–42.

Turnley, W., Bolino, M., Lester, S., & Bloodgood, J. (2003). The impact of psychological contract fulfillment on the performance of in-role and organizational citizenship behaviors. *Journal of Management*, *29*, 187–206.

Weick, K. E. (1995). *Sensemaking in organizations* (vol. 3). Thousand Oaks, CA: Sage.

Whitney, D., Cooperrider, D., Trosten-Bloom, A., & Kaplin, B. S. (2002). *Encyclopedia of positive questions.* Euclid, OH: Lakeshore Communications.

Whitney, D., & Trosten-Bloom, A. (2003). *The power of appreciative inquiry.* San Francisco: Berrett Koehler.

Wilke, D. (2017). *Miserable modern workers: Why are they so unhappy?* SHRM. https://www.shrm.org/topics-tools/news/employee-relations/miserable-modern-workers-unhappy.

Wilson, D., & Williams, V. (2013). Ubuntu: Development and framework of a specific model of positive mental health. *Psychology Journal*, *10*(2), 80–100.

Wren, D. A., & Bedeian, A. G. (2020). *The evolution of management thought.* (8th ed) Hoboken, NJ: John Wiley & Sons.

Wright Mills, C. (1959). *The sociological imagination*. New York: Oxford University Press

Zipay, K. P., Pychlau, S., & Wagner, D. T. (2020, August 7–11). Third places and workplace outcomes. In R. Livne-Tarandach & H. Jazaieri (Eds.), *New frontiers of community research.* Symposium conducted at the annual meeting of the Academy of Management.

Index

For the benefit of digital users, indexed terms that span two pages (e.g., 52–53) may, on occasion, appear on only one of those pages.